THIRD EDITION

The Prophets

Strategies & Training in the School of the Spirit

STEVEN FRANCIS

Published by:
Steven Francis Ministries
409 Polkville Road, Shelby, North Carolina 28150, USA.

Email: info@riversapostolic.com
www.riversapostolic.com

This book's first edition – God's Special Force – ISBN: 981-05-6782-0
Second Revised Edition – The Prophets – ISBN: 978-9-811107-21-4
Third Edition – The Prophets – ISBN: 978-1-949106-74-9

DEDICATION

I dedicate this book to Him who was, who is, and who is to come, my precious Lord and Savior, Jesus Christ, God, the Blessed and only Ruler, the King of kings and Lord of lords, who alone is immortal and who lives in unapproachable light, whom no one has seen or can see—to Him be honor and might forever. Amen.

To my elder brother and spiritual father, Sadhu Sundar Selvaraj, who has served the Lord for the past forty years, tirelessly, sacrificially, dying to self, bearing the cross, whose lifestyle of prayer, faith, and an intimate walk with God, qualities I admire, cherish, and learn from; he is a general in the Lord's end-time army.

To the students and alumni of The King's College of Prophets, into whom I have imparted and taught the wisdom of the Lord, may you be empowered by the love of God to walk with Jesus, to serve His purpose, and live for His glory.

To my children, may you each become the prophetic voice to your generation.

WORD TO OPERATIONALLY READY WARRIORS OF CHRIST:

The Darkest Hour
that is about to fall on us, the Church,
will be the finest moment
in the history of the Kingdom of God.

Always be ready!
The sound of the trumpet has been heard.
Risking all, we must fight for Him
who died for us, Jesus, our Lord!

We are going to see Him as He is!

Chief Commander, the Lord of Hosts,
the King of kings and
the Lord of lords!

Battalion,
we will soon meet each other
on the other side, in heaven!

Live only for His glory!

CONTENTS

ACKNOWLEDGMENTS

I wish to heartily thank a team of people who have been involved in this project. I want to thank my wife, Pastor Angeline Francis, who encouraged me through this process.

I'd like to thank my administrative staff team of Jesus My King Church for their constant encouragement to complete this third edition book.

Design and layout support was provided by Isaac Chew, who knows how to respond to all last-minute projects and who does an excellent job for the Lord.

Special thanks to Brother Tom Rutherford for encouraging me for this first USA print project and Dr. Roberts Liardon for writing the foreword for this new edition.

FOREWORD

BY DR. ROBERTS LIARDON

My heart connects with Steven Francis's purpose behind writing *The Prophets,* because it's closely aligned to the mandate God has placed on my own life: to help raise up a new generation of bold, sold-out leaders, ready to invade the nations with the Gospel in the power of the Spirit. Steven addresses the matter of God's end-time army, bringing his own uniquely powerful gifts of prophetic insight and revelation to a message that Heaven introduced to the Body of Christ more than a generation ago.

Steven states: "The Lord has already decreed the release of the end-time army. This army will be greatly assisted by the supernatural army of heaven to bring judgment on the nations and to usher in the Second Coming of Jesus Christ." This book serves as a powerful prophetic training tool for those leaders in the Body who need to wake up to the fact they have already been recruited and get serious about the business of training to effectively advance the Kingdom.

As I read these pages, I was reminded of a prophetic word I heard through Brother Kenneth E. Hagin as a youth when I spent so many hours listening to his teaching. I remember back in the 1970s when Brother Hagin prophesied more than once about God's "new breed" army...

"...And know ye this, that the Lord has an army.

Yea, He is preparing His own.

No, the Church will not grow weaker and weaker and weaker and lie down and expire.

But she shall grow stronger and stronger and stronger, for a fresh visitation of Heaven is at hand...

And so men, some would call them a "NEW BREED," shall rise up and go forth.

They shall not be afraid of the devil.

They shall have no fear of men.

But with boldness shall they speak and shall challenge the very strongholds of the devil...."

—Kenneth E. Hagin, 1975

By the time you finish reading this book, you'll know that you're already working through a divine training course to prepare you to take your place in this end-time army and bring your full supply to the battle. As a seasoned commander in God's prophetic "special forces," Steven offers a rich store of experience and knowledge of both the enemy's tactics and the Commander in Chief's strategic plans of operation. This book will help equip and fortify you for the battles that lay ahead—battles that you are destined to *win*!

Dr. Roberts Liardon
Author of the *God's Generals* Series
Sarasota, Florida

INTRODUCTION

Be Operationally Ready!

I sat with my family in a church for one Sunday service. As they introduced the guest preacher, I took my pen and notebook out, ready to take notes of his sermon.

Right at that moment, the Spirit of God birthed a prayer within my spirit: *Lord, I pray for the revelation of the 7,000 company.* While I listened to the speaker with my natural ears, my spiritual ears were decoding a message from the Holy Spirit.

Right then, the revelation of the Spirit of God filled my heart, and I wrote the outline of this book. I believe this message is a timely message for the Body of Christ, for ministers and prayer warriors.

The enemy has released many flares to send smoke toward the people of God and the undiscerning believers in order to camouflage his strategies against the Church. However, he will fail! The eyes of the Lord are watching all evil in every place (Proverbs 15:3). We will stand in His name against the works of the enemy. Many (but not all) servants of God have been enticed by the enemy with riches, power, and earthly fame to sell their birthright of covenant blessings. Like Balaam, some have settled down for the cheaper riches of this earth instead of pursuing heavenly riches.

Some, who have been called by God to possess the spirit of a warrior for this end-time showdown, have become weary and have disqualified themselves from the training in the school of the Spirit. Some have allowed the sword of the Spirit in their hearts to become so blunt and dull as their hearts have become hardened. No revelation can touch a hardened heart unless you know the truth (Mark 8:17–18).

Some, like Samson, are involved with the wrong ministries in the wrong places at the wrong time. They may seem satisfied that they are doing certain types of ministry, and they may even be producing visible results. However, little do they know that the enemy has enticed them away from fulfilling their true purpose according to the will of God.

My brothers and sisters, are you serving under a pharisaical leadership that prevents you from serving the call of God? You may ask me, "How can I know if I am under such leadership?" If the leadership imposes fear and intimidation on you, and as a result you seek to please them above God, then a pharisaical spirit is in operation. Unless you choose to break free, you will never be able to serve God's call in your life.

In recent times, there has been a stirring in my heart with regard to combating this spirit of control within the Body of Christ, which we will discuss later in this book.

Once again, I heard the sound of the trumpet while I was praying, and I heard the Lord say that the time is short, and that His angels are active in preparing for the Second Coming of Jesus.

JOEL 2:1 NKJV

Blow the trumpet in Zion, and sound an alarm in My holy mountain! Let all the inhabitants of the land tremble; for the day of the LORD is coming, for it is at hand.

We should no longer be quiet in the Spirit and endure unnecessary intimidation of the enemy. I desire to set the trumpet of the Lord's voice to my mouth (Hosea 8:1) and sound the alarm to your spirit. Arise and gather in the name of Jesus. I command every mental stronghold over your mind and the dullness in your mind to be broken in Jesus' name.

You are invited and called to be a part of the remnant in the Body of Christ. He wants to anoint you afresh and use you. Do not brush off the holy stirrings of the Holy Spirit in your heart.

LET GOD ARISE

PSALM 68:1–3 NKJV

Let God arise, let His enemies be scattered; let those also who hate Him flee before Him. As smoke is driven away, so drive them away; as wax melts before the fire, so let the wicked perish at the presence of God. But let the righteous be glad; let them rejoice before God; yes, let them rejoice exceedingly.

Keep honoring God in your life. Exalt Him and magnify His grace and His calling in your life. Stand up for Him. Do not fear what man can do to you. Surely the Lord will scatter the enemies who have surrounded you to pull you down.

The word *arise* is fascinating in the Hebrew language. It comes from the Hebrew word *qum*, which means to stand up, to engage in battle, to continue something, to rise again, and to commit to the beginning of an action.

Consistency Builds Momentum

From my interaction with many ministers who are mature and deep in the knowledge of God's ways, I have discovered some essential spiritual disciplines that are constant in their lives. They are consistent in their walk **in** Christ and **for** Christ (Mark 3:14). Consistency builds momentum in our walk with Christ. Let me just share with you some of these pointers.

Build your life strong in the Word and prayer, as these two supernatural disciplines will arm you with strength for the battle (Psalm 18:39; 119:28; Ephesians 6:10). Continue to walk and live in Christ (Colossians 1:23); walk in faith (Colossians 1:23); and remain steadfast in the things you have learned from the Lord through His Word (2 Timothy 3:14).

Walk in forgiveness—not only forgiving others but also forgiving yourself. The Bible says, "For a righteous man may fall seven times and rise again, but the wicked shall fall by calamity" (Proverbs 24:16 NKJV). No matter what struggles you may be going through, no matter how discouraged you have become, pick yourself up and shout at the enemy this promise from the book of Micah:

MICAH 7:8–10

Do not gloat over me, my enemy! Though I have fallen, I will rise. Though I sit in darkness, the LORD will be my light. Because I have sinned against him, I will bear the LORD's wrath until he pleads my case and establishes my right. He will bring me out into the light; I will see his righteousness. Then my enemy will see it and will be covered with shame, she who said to me, "Where is the LORD your God?" My eyes will see her downfall; even now she will be trampled underfoot like mire in the streets.

Like Jacob, wrestle with the Lord for your victory (Genesis 32:22–31). Prevail in the Spirit over time. This prevailing will build your spiritual stamina, consistency, and intimacy with the Lord. Victory is not for the careless, the inconsistent, or those who are plain lazy in the flesh. The enemy is frightened of you. He knows what the anointing can do to his works and his kingdom through you. The anointing has the capacity to destroy all the yokes of bondage that the devil is throwing across your path (Isaiah 10:27). You are God's special force!

You are trained by the Holy Spirit to walk through all types of terrain. Let there be waters, the Lord is with you; let there be rivers, you know they will not overflow; and when you walk through the fire, you will not be burned or scorched, nor will the flame be kindled upon you (Isaiah 43:2).

EPHESIANS 6:11 AMPC

Put on God's whole armor [the armor of a heavy-armed soldier which God supplies], that you may be able successfully to stand up against [all] the strategies and the deceits of the devil.

I want to shout out aloud with the prophet Isaiah against the host of darkness: "Devise your strategy, but it will be thwarted; propose your plan, but it will not stand, for God is with us" (Isaiah 8:10).

My brethren in Christ, these are the days when we are going to witness the supernatural ability of the Lord enabling His army to walk in His power and fulfill His purpose. Let us stand shoulder to shoulder with our chest up and look straight at Jesus.

ISAIAH 19:3 AMPC

And the spirit of the Egyptians within them will become exhausted and emptied out and will fail, and I will destroy their counsel and confound their plans, and they will seek counsel from the idols and the sorcerers, and from those having familiar spirits (the mediums) and the wizards.

Another Bible translation of this verse reads, "*Then the spirit of the Egyptians will be demoralized within them, and I will confound their strategy*" (NASB).

ISAIAH 13:3–5 NASB

I have commanded My consecrated ones, I have even called My mighty warriors, My proudly exulting ones, to execute My anger.

A sound of tumult on the mountains, like that of many people! A sound of the uproar of kingdoms, of nations gathered together! The LORD *of hosts is mustering the army for battle.*

They are coming from a far country, from the farthest horizons, the LORD *and His instruments of indignation, to destroy the whole land.*

The Lord has already decreed the release of the end-time army. This army will be greatly assisted by the supernatural army of heaven to bring judgment on the nations and to usher in the Second Coming of Jesus Christ.

It is time for the Church to strike back. No more defensive strategies. Envy and jealousy in the Church must stop. Do not take your eyes off the real enemy. It is time to aim and hit at the right target. Don't waste your time hunting down clones.

We are men and women of honor, fighting for one cause and one purpose. Don't let the flag of Jesus down. Hold it up and fight until the last breath. We will bring Satan and his strategies down in Jesus' name! Take your orders and march on, soldier!

SECOND EDITION

Little did I know what the Lord's plans were for my life from the first edition of this book. The messages in this book contain the lessons the Lord taught me when He allowed me to walk through the wilderness for three years. He spoke to me that "from 2006 to 2009, will be your wilderness walk. After 2009, I will restore all that the locusts have eaten."

In my mind, I thought the book was a result of the personal challenges and controversies that were permitted by heaven. I did not know that I had to go through another three years of wilderness. Out of that walk in the dark, the Lord Jesus became my light.

In the year 2010, during a trip to Jerusalem, I had divine encounters from heaven. The Lord instructed me, together with my wife, to launch the King's College of Prophets to train the prophetic army for this end-time harvest. Through the college, the Lord said He would raise up His prophets. A few months later, the King's College of Prophets was birthed by the Lord. Soon to follow, the Lord told me to start a church, and all prophetic mission trips and conferences were restored.

The resurrection life of Jesus came into my spirit, and with the strength and encouragement of my wife, Angeline, and the ministry team, we are raising up an army for the Lord. All the lessons learned in the secret place of the Most High became the subjects taught in the King's College of Prophets.

The Lord is faithful to His promises. All wilderness training is accompanied by the Holy Spirit and the angels of God. This last-days army must pass the wilderness test. If you are going through your moments now, do not lose heart. The Lord will lift you up. Do not be afraid to surrender your life, family, and ministry to the Lord. He restores everything.

Your fellow soldier in His troop,
God's Special Force

Steven and Angeline Francis
August 2016 Singapore

THIRD EDITION

I had a powerful encounter with the Lord Jesus Christ on November 2018. I will write here, in brief, about this encounter. While I was in the Los Angeles International Airport, I saw the glory of God in a visible light. When I lifted up my head, I heard a strong, loud bass tone voice. I knew in my spirit; this was the voice of the Father. Three times before, I have heard the audible voice of the Father. It is a voice of authority that will even make your bones shiver.

The voice of the Father said, "I want you to move to North Carolina." I received the words in my heart. When I reached home in Singapore, I told my wife what the Lord said. It was about three in the morning. I commented to her, "The Lord said North Carolina, but where in this place does He want us to go?"

The moment I said those words, the Lord Jesus appeared as a burning fire, but I could see His whole person beside me. The fear of the Lord gripped me. My wife was looking at Google Maps on the iPad. The Lord's right hand moved across my chest. He said to me, "I will give you your first sign. What is the name of your church?" Jesus asked me. I said, "Lord, You know, Jesus My King." He then gestured me to tell my wife, Angeline, to swipe the iPad from left to right once. I saw the finger of Jesus showing me exactly what she was supposed to do.

When she did that, the map moved and stopped at Kings Mountain, North Carolina. Tears filled my eyes. The fear of the Lord gripped my soul. On the third day of my arrival back home, similarly, the Lord Jesus appeared to me in the same manner and told me the address of the property I should buy.

I kept these matters in my heart. My wife and I were troubled in our hearts as we did not know what God was asking us to do clearly. Our children were studying in Singapore. The church and The King's College of Prophets were growing. Our annual conferences were expanding. How would I share this with my elders and leaders in church?

During December 2018, my wife and I fasted for fourteen days. On the first day of the fast, at about three in the morning, I heard the audible voice of the Lord Jesus. He said, "Come up." At once, my spirit was caught up in heaven. There I saw a wide, big, open land. I saw a saint standing there, and he gestured me to come towards him. When I went towards him, he introduced himself to me, "My name is Abraham. Follow me." I walked for some distance, and the saint Abraham said, "The Lord wants you to shift your base to the new land which the Father has shown you. You must not delay. This is your next assignment from the Father. You are to go to this new place to prepare a place for the end-time remnant whom the Lord Himself will assemble."

Through the fourteen days of fasting and prayer, I was caught up into heaven as the Lord gave me instructions on how I should handle this transition. The Lord worked out everything for us. It was not easy emotionally to leave behind our family, children, church members whom we have invested our lives into, and friends we grew up with. Nevertheless, we count it as an honor to be trusted by heaven in this new assignment.

The Lord gave me more confirmations—angelic assistance and miraculous providence, to name a few—to confirm the Word of the Lord.

The message in this book is more important now than the time I wrote it in 2006. Now is the time for the remnant to rise up.

As you are holding this book, may the anointing of God come upon you as you digest the pages of this book in your spirit. The Lord will launch you in the spirit as you consecrate your life for the cause of God.

In a short period of one year, during Covid-19, we launched Jesus My King Church, and she is growing. We launched The King's College of Prophets, and the Lord is blessing the work.

The Lord Jesus spoke to me again about His second coming and the judgments to come. We need to prepare our hearts and walk in the Word and in the Spirit. The armies of the Lord are not a confused bunch. The armies of the Lord, filled with the Holy Spirit, are directed by the Lord. They know where they are going. They know how to follow instructions. They are not lost soldiers.

Many in the church are wondering what the Lord's will for them is. Without discipline in the matters of God, how would anyone be enlisted in the army of the Lord? Be resolved in your heart to keep in step with the Spirit.

An army of Elijahs is rising. These will be anointed to flow in the supernatural miracles of God. They will speak the Word with power and boldness. Physical signs of the glory of God will manifest to authenticate their anointing and calling.

Rise up, Church. God is counting on you to complete the work of Jesus on earth!

Steven and Angeline Francis
June 2022
North Carolina, USA

OPS BRIEFING 1

BATTLE PLANS OF THE ENEMY

I have been through my share of spiritual battles, just like any other servant of God. The Lord Jesus permitted these times of trials and testing. The Lord has allowed me, by His direct supervision, to see high-ranking demons that control certain geographical regions for the purpose of prayer and deliverance.

Some years back, I was scheduled to preach in a church in Ulladulla, New South Wales, Australia. I had never met the pastor before, nor did I know any details about his ministry. As I was preparing for these two night sessions, the Lord revealed the work of a high-controlling demon in that town. I am sure this is not news to you, as we all know demons are everywhere and that they are permitted to operate in various areas. So, what was so special about this town?

The Lord showed me that a spirit of adultery, together with the spirit of Jezebel, was controlling that area. The Lord told me to address those issues in the church. I understand how painful it is for a pastor when a visiting speaker reveals problems about his church shown to him by the Spirit of God. The pastor would be embarrassed that someone knew what was going on, or he could be thanking Jesus that God had sent someone to deal with the prevailing problem. In this church, it was the latter. The pastor and the leadership rejoiced that God had sent a prophet to them.

During the second night service, the anointing of God was strong on me. I preached a message titled "Overcoming Demonic Powers." The presence of God visited the service. Many people responded to the altar call in repentance for giving room to the spirit of adultery, which had ruined their marital lives. Apparently, according to the senior pastor of the church, one of his pastoral team elders had run away with another married woman in the church. This act of adultery had affected the spiritual standing of the church considerably.

That Sunday afternoon, the Holy Spirit brought His cleansing power to the church. There was much repentance and tears among the people. The pastoral team and the congregation thankfully worshiped the Lord for His goodness to His people.

On another occasion, I was scheduled to preach in a Combined Churches Intercessors Seminar. This was in Beenleigh, Queensland, Australia. I had not met the pastors before. While the worship was going on, I began to pray. I could smell dried chile peppers. As I took a deep breath, there was a burning sensation in my chest. I wondered how it was possible to have the smell of dried chile peppers in an Aussie church. I walked to the back of the church just to check around if there was any. I did not find any. I came to the front and continued worshiping the Lord.

When I closed my eyes, my spirit left my body and looked at the left side of the window. There was a man; he told me he was the local warlock who had been placing curses on the churches around. He told me that the demons told him that I was coming to minister in the church. The warlock came to see me by "soul travel."

After the warlock left, I began to seek the Lord. The Spirit of the Lord came upon me, and I was taken in the spirit into a forest. I was traveling slow enough through the forest that I could see different things in the woods. Figurines of idols were at different corners of the pathway. Some were birds like owls that represented the monitoring spirits that would see and give information to the warlock and witches. As I continued on the pathway, I was brought to a black castle-like house. On top of this house were two phoenix birds and a dragon statue. When I looked at the window, the warlock was standing right there and looked straight at me.

The Lord brought me back into my body and spoke to me audibly. He revealed to me how the warlock had cast curses on the churches and pastors. I saw a spirit of infirmity and confusion placed over the churches. I shared this revelation and began to pray much with the people. Some of them were receptive, while others were skeptical.

The next day, the Assemblies of God pastor, whom I stayed with, brought me to breakfast. He said, "First, let me bring you to another location to show you something." The pastor drove to a lonely pathway in the forest, and there was the warlock's house as it was in my spiritual encounter. During breakfast, the pastor explained how each of the pastors in the town was suffering from major illnesses, and the churches were constantly experiencing problems with the congregation. He was thankful that the Lord brought me there to reveal the demonic works and break the power of witchcraft.

The question remains, "Why didn't the church have any power in prayer?" Prayer without the power of the Holy Spirit goes nowhere. When the fire of God is not present in the hearts of the people, even demons are not afraid. Soulish prayers are not effective in the realm of darkness. Prayers by people who lack godliness will do little in the spiritual realm. Many times, I have witnessed soulish people praying that have no power. Their prayers do not change their own lives. Praying people will experience constant change by the Holy Spirit. The spirit of godliness will transform them from inside. They will see their old habits and patterns of thoughts are dying, and the new patterns of thoughts shaped by the Word are taking root.

Before engaging in spiritual warfare, ensure that you are filled with the power of the Holy Spirit. You are baptized in the Spirit. Come under the blood of the Lamb. Walk in love. Remove all the roots of bitterness. If not, the spirit of flattery will mask and use you as an instrument of confusion.

I want to encourage you: if God has not authorized you to engage in spiritual warfare against territorial demons or warlocks, then please do not engage out of curiosity. Stay within the limits of your spiritual authority. The more you grow in the Lord, the greater will be the strength of your inner man. As per the leading of the Holy Spirit, engage in warfare. The rule of thumb is: engage demonic powers that are against you and your family first before engaging in spiritual warfare against the town. Demons can recognize true prayer warriors and bogus ones. Stand on the safe side.

VISION OF AN UNWANTED SPIRIT

In February 2003, I went to South India to pray with a man of God for some important matters concerning my life and ministry. The Lord uses this dear servant of God as a prophet with profound supernatural experiences. We knelt together in prayer, and the Spirit of the Lord came upon this brother, and he prophesied for two hours. I want to include a brief note of that prophecy.

During prayer in the month of February 2003, the Lord revealed the operation of a very high-level, feminine demonic stronghold. She is a terrible spirit that seeks to decrease men through deceit. She will weaken and confuse their hearts. She operates through the veins and muscles in order to steal their strength.

She is a spirit of prostitution, an unclean spirit. Her aim is to destroy ministries that are critical for the last days. The body of this spirit was disgusting to behold. It was many-breasted. The many breasts are a symbol of the many operations under her wings. Many organizations will be under her control and will receive direct support from her. This spirit will have the power to sow seeds and confuse men's hormone systems. It will destroy the immune system and potentially release new, previously unknown strains of viruses that will destroy their immune system. We are witnessing the release of many new strains of unknown diseases that are taking the scientists by surprise. The Lord's counsel is for His church to pray for everyone's protection from these attacks. This spirit's goal is to plant one of her operations in the islands to the east of Singapore.

The manifesto of this spirit expresses itself and operates through:

- Medicine (tablets), drugs, ecstasy pills, etc.
- The fashion industry to inspire vanity and fornication
- Books
- Cinema
- Music
- The toilet (possibly unclean and hidden places)
- Places of business

Men will build secret places of worship for this spirit. Little children will become exposed, and some will become carriers of this spirit.

Some cult groups will host secret, ritualistic worship services at places near the sea and high places on the mountains, which will become places of sacrifices for this spirit. The Lord showed me the regions of America and England. Babies will be sacrificed to empower this spirit. There is *anger* in the eyes of this spirit. As a dragon, smoke comes from her nostrils, and fire shoots from her mouth. In the coming days, terrible things lie ahead of us. Young people and children will be tainted by this spirit.

At the time of this third edition, the Lord has shown me more secret places of satanic strongholds. I have been brought in the spirit to one location in Africa, one island in South America, and one beach island in the Philippines. As we warfare in the spirit, these strongholds are shaken of their power. The moment their curses are not effective, the warlocks take note and will send demonic spirits to investigate the cause of the interruption.

In October 2018, I was in Manila, Philippines, together with my elder brother Sadhu Sundar Selvaraj. I was invited by him to teach in his School of Prophets. During one of the sessions, as I led in spiritual warfare for this nation, I was caught up in the spirit. The Lord brought me in the spirit to an island. The angel of the Lord and I were hovering just above the island. I was shown a cave where naked young women were there as sex slaves with a young man possessed by Lucifer. He has sex with these girls, and their fetuses are sacrificed to Satan. These girls looked up as they knew something was above them but could not see us. When this young man came out, he saw me directly. This young man possessed by Lucifer could see in the spirit realm. The Lord spoke to me that the young man knows his victory would be short-lived. I was brought back to the church and continued prayer.

JOURNAL OF THE UNKNOWN PROPHET

I came across a book entitled *Journal of the Unknown Prophet,*[1] written by Wendy Alec. She had a supernatural encounter with the

[1] Wendy Alec, *Journal of the Unknown Prophet* (Warboys Media, 2002), 257.

Lord. In this book, the Lord revealed to her the end-time attacks of the enemy.

"And suddenly it was as though a heavy, heavenly veil was drawn back in the spirit realm, and I saw the satanic princes in their battle dress standing in their chariots, directing the great mass of hellish battalions and powers and principalities, and they were standing as a great and seemingly fearsome mass in a line that stretched to eternity, waiting. And then a great shofar was sounded, and the fallen satanic princes and generals took their places in front of the battalions, as the great rumbling of Satan's chariots thundered. And as one, they bowed their heads—as the Prince of Darkness made his entrance.

"And as he stood there—all terrible in his damnable arrogance and rebellion—he lifted his sword high to the heavenly, and again, as one man, I saw the princes and their battalions follow suit, and I heard Lucifer's spine-chilling cry: 'It is *time*!' And the hordes of hell resounded with a great and terrible cry: 'It is *time*.' And as Lucifer turned to his fallen princes, I could hear his malicious hiss: *'It is time to target the champions!'*"

MINISTERS UNDER ATTACK

The Lord revealed to me that ministers would be under aggressive attack by Satan. He is after those who walk in obedience to the will of God. He is angry with those who are fervent in their spirits to fulfill the ministry God has set for them.

Satan has targeted the families and marriages of ministers. His plan is to destroy the spiritual seed that will produce a God-fearing generation of soul winners who will destroy the works of the enemy. The enemy plans to bring interruptions into ministers' families. Stand strong, soldier—when God is with you, who can be against you? (Deuteronomy 33:29; Psalm 27:1–3; Romans 8:31).

During my time of fasting and prayer in 2006, the Lord again permitted me to have an encounter with this spirit. I saw the eyes of Jezebel looking at my family. At once, I began to fast and pray to secure the spiritual perimeters of my family with the blood of Jesus and with warring angels. Continue to press on to walk in the true anointing of the Lord. I encourage you to read my book, *The Anointing & the Fragrance*. In this book, I wrote how the Lord showed me that Jezebel would use the weapon of flattery and false anointing to bring defeat into the lives of ministers and the body of Christ.

The spirit of Jezebel will continue to fight those who have the ability to see in the realm of the spirit (1 Kings 18:4). These ministers are a threat to her, as they know her tactical moves by the Lord's revelation.

One of her many tactics is to forge false and purposeless unity among ministers. The pastors will seem to gather often, but their spirits will be under a "spiritual coma." There will be no revelation in their spirits, and prophets will be kept out of their circles.

If the Kingdom of God is to greatly advance, there must be more praying than feasting. There must be more fasting in the Upper Room than feasting in the supper room.

My minister friends, if you don't keep your spirit man in shape by walking in the will of God and in discernment, the enemy will tempt you to become a religious leader with a pharisaical spirit. Instead of becoming a watchman of the Lord and keeping the fortress from the enemy's invasion, you will end up standing against the prophets and the spirit of revelation.

I am discharging these warnings to you and the Body of Christ as per the Lord's instructions. Be warned ahead of time. I wrote this book after agonizing on my knees in prayer and fasting for three years.

Another attack from the enemy is the spirit of offense we can foster against one another. Once, when I was in Australia for two weeks of ministry, I had a dream. I was sitting in a living room, and the top corners of the house were decorated with aboriginal paintings of Australia. Many of the paintings had demonic symbols[2] on them.

Then I saw a pastor from Singapore enter in through the front door and sit on the sofa. I stood up. I had an axe in my right hand. I was overwhelmed with anger, and I swung the axe across his head. The axe got stuck in his head, and blood was everywhere.

I jumped out of my bed, awakened from this unbelievable dream. My heart was pounding so fast, as though I had really murdered someone. I began to pray with much burden, although it was four o'clock in the morning with freezing temperatures. I

---

2 Not all aboriginal paintings are demonic. You need to really discern in the Spirit. This was a dream the Lord showed me.

told the Lord that I do not harbor any murderous offenses against anyone. I asked Him to show me the meaning of the dream.

And the Lord spoke to me. He told me that the spirit of offense would release a murderous spirit against the ministers. Close friends will begin to pick up offenses by giving in to this spirit, and they will kill each other's ministries and anointing. Unless we walk in love, we will become unaware of this satanic strategy.

THE PLAN AGAINST OUR CHILDREN

In the year 1998, I was invited to speak at a Combined Leaders and Intercessors Prayer Seminar in Brisbane, Australia. Before I was about to go and teach, the Lord showed me many visions. I want to share with you one of them that concerns the enemy's plans against our children.

I saw a vision of two boys playing by the side of a big river. The bigger boy pushed the smaller lad into the river. I saw a demon standing behind the bigger boy, looking down at the drowning boy with a demonic smile.

On January 30, 1999, there was a report in the *Straits Times* (in Singapore) of an Aussie boy from Sydney who was charged with manslaughter. He was "accused of dropping a struggling six-year-old into a river and leaving him to drown," just as I had seen in the vision.

The Holy Spirit revealed to me that in these last days, the demonic attacks against our children will increase. There is a demonic ambition to stop them from becoming the end-time army of God.

I wrote an article for our ministry magazine, *Harvest Glory,* in 1999. The Lord revealed, "Children will arise in My name and do miracles. Younger people will respond to the call of God. This is the generation of the young."

PSALM 8:2 NKJV

Out of the mouth of babes and nursing infants You have ordained strength, because of Your enemies, that You may silence the enemy and the avenger.

Children are going to play pivotal roles in these end times. They will be anointed by the Lord Jesus to see visions and prophesy (Joel 2:28). The anointing of God will flow tangibly through them, as their hearts are pure and right before Him. They do not care for their own names to be known, nor do they speak with pride. Their shyness will become their very strength as they hide behind the cross of Christ to minister.

I remember a group of young children who came to pray for me while I was in Brisbane, Australia. This was my first experience with children in ministry. These children were used by the Lord to prophesy and see visions. Some expressed themselves through coloring—and each color was spiritually significant to me. Others expressed themselves through drawing on paper the visions they saw while in prayer. Some girls expressed themselves through prophetic drawings, while a young boy prophesied, "Thus saith the Lord..."

It was mind-blowing to me. All the prophecies, pictures, colors, and songs were exact and accurate. Senior prophets had also given many of these prophecies to me, and some were the Lord's revelation to me while in prayer. It was just awesome!

Shortly afterward, I heard that a new pastor who was an "anti-prophecy" pastor had taken over the church. He dismantled this prophetic kids' ministry and banned them from meeting and praying in their private homes or in the church. How sad!

MY SON, SAMUEL JOHN, PROPHESIED OVER ME

My elder brother prophesied that God would give me a son who would be sensitive to the workings of God and that he would carry the call of God on his life. The Lord named my son Samuel John—one who would be sensitive to the voice of God and who would become an end-time messenger. Samuel John was born on September 24, 1998.

Many times, my son shared with me that he had seen Jesus calling him and assuring him that the Lord would continue to bless our family. At times, he has heard the voice of Jesus calling him, "Samuel, Samuel."

But this one time was different. I was going through the most difficult period of my life. Many months were spent travailing in prayer and tears. Usually, I would be in the kids' room praying while they played outside.

On this night, my son wanted to sit beside me while I was in prayer. Suddenly, he just started to sing a Christian song in the Tamil language, which is a South Indian language. He kept on singing a particular verse, repeating it about ten times. For a moment, I thought he was interrupting me in his childlikeness. Just then, I heard the voice of Jesus say, *"I am speaking to you through your son, and you are not paying attention."*

I stopped praying and told Samuel to sing again. The lyrics of the song were: "Though I can hear a million voices discouraging, one word from Jesus is all that I need." That was the word of the Lord to me. Why was it so amazing? At that time, Samuel could not speak the Tamil language fluently. Whenever I talked to him in Tamil, Samuel would reply in English. But on that afternoon, he sang the lines of this song in perfect Tamil. That was just too much to handle!

My daughter Samantha is also sensitive in the Spirit. She picks up a tune of a worship song and flows along. May God continue to bless and use them both! Revival history records many children having prophetic encounters.[3] The Lord used them to prophesy over the adults. This is the fulfillment of the prophet Joel's prophecy.

ANGELS LIKE CHILDREN

While I was ministering in a church, the Lord graced my eyes to see little angels. Their features were that of children. The Holy Spirit gave me the insight that it was His desire to bless the children

---

3 http://www.kidsinministry.com/PropheticChildren.html

present in the meetings. As such, the power of God came upon the children in a mighty way.

On another occasion, while in worship of the Lord, by His grace, I was allowed to have a supernatural visitation to a place in heaven. It was a very beautiful garden. Trees were everywhere, and I saw beautiful flowers all around. I saw children playing. The entire episode was like music to my ears. The noises the children made merged into a beautiful symphony. Then I saw angels instructing children about the Bible and the life of Christ. That is where they are being nurtured to grow in the knowledge of Jesus.

My precious parents, if you have lost your baby or child or know someone who has, please know this: God is taking good care of your children. They are being watched over and taught by the angels of God.

PROTECT YOUR CHILDREN

Be watchful over your children in the natural as well as in the Spirit. Pray for them that the Lord will show you things about them through dreams, visions, or prophecies. Have their eternity in mind as you train them up to grow in life.

Just as Pharaoh commanded the male children to be cast into the river out of fear of a coming deliverer (Exodus 1:22), and just as Herod, being afraid of a new king (Matthew 2:16), commanded that all male babies under the age of two be killed, so Satan has launched a strong and fearsome attack against our children.

Our Lord Jesus is raising up children in these last days for His glory. They are going to grow up strong in the Spirit, built up by the Word. They will stand against the host of darkness through prayer. These children will become mighty giants in the Body of Christ. Bring your child up in the ways of the Lord. Our children will face the world and the challenges. They need to experience Jesus as their Savior. They will be exposed to the wiles and temptations of this present age. God will protect our children.

BE SERIOUS IN YOUR MIND

1 PETER 4:7 NKJV

But the end of all things is at hand; therefore be serious and watchful in your prayers.

The word *serious* comes from the Greek word *sophroneo*, meaning "to be of sound mind or to be in a right mind." The Holy Spirit is forewarning His people of how it shall be in these last days that the minds of people will be overloaded with the cares of this world, which will then choke the Word of God out of their lives.

MARK 4:18–19 AMPC

And the ones sown among the thorns are others who hear the Word; then the cares and anxieties of the world and distractions of the age, and the pleasure and delight and false glamour and deceitfulness of riches, and the craving and passionate desire for other things creep in and choke and suffocate the Word, and it becomes fruitless.

Even seemingly religious activities in Christian circles could become so overloaded with meetings that they distract believers' attention away from the Lord. We cannot be watchful in the Spirit with an overloaded life and an overcrowded mind. Pull out the weeds of busyness. Check the influences around you, the type of people with whom you are surrounded and the types of conversation with which your mind is filled.

Some of us must learn how to wait upon the Lord again. Let your mind be free from the world and its influences and be filled instead with the conscious presence of the Lord (Matthew 22:37).

EPHESIANS 4:17–19, 22–24 AMPC

So this I say and solemnly testify in [the name of] the Lord [as in His presence], that you must no longer live as the heathen (the Gentiles) do in their perverseness [in the folly, vanity, and emptiness of their souls and the futility] of their minds.

Their moral understanding is darkened and their reasoning is beclouded. [They are] alienated (estranged, self-banished) from the life of God [with no share in it; this is] because of the ignorance (the want of knowledge and perception, the willful blindness) that is deep-seated in them, due to their hardness of heart [to the insensitiveness of their moral nature].

In their spiritual apathy they have become callous and past feeling and reckless and have abandoned themselves [a prey] to unbridled sensuality, eager and greedy to indulge in every form of impurity [that their depraved desires may suggest and demand].

Strip yourselves of your former nature [put off and discard your old unrenewed self] which characterized your previous manner of life and becomes corrupt through lusts and desires that spring from delusion;

And be constantly renewed in the spirit of your mind [having a fresh mental and spiritual attitude],

And put on the new nature (the regenerate self) created in God's image, [Godlike] in true righteousness and holiness.

If you have walked out of your calling, I urge you, my beloved, to repent from your ways and get back to Jesus. The enemy wants to feed your mind with falsehoods about the things of God; to keep your mind focused on people who have disappointed you; to keep your mind trapped by unanswered prayers or the death of your loved ones. Satan will do his best to keep your heart, soul, and mind angered toward God, thereby cutting off the life flow of God's power to your spirit.

The process of backsliding away from the life of God will be so subtle that you will not even realize that your spirit has become dry. You will tend to adopt new activities to fill the dryness of your heart. Your heart will start to become cold and desensitized from the warmth of the presence of God. Your mind will be far from comprehending the things of God, and your heart will begin to harden. Impurity and greed will invade your heart, and the very things of this world that you thought you could handle will become a snare to your soul.

From being a consistent child of God, you will settle for being a "once in a while" believer, attending the house of God at your convenience. Do you know what is happening inside you? The lack of the fear of God has entered your heart. Your very smart and intelligent reasoning power will become the graveyard that buries your destiny and your calling in Christ.

In fact, one of the many strategies of warfare is called *psychological warfare*. During times of war, a nation may spread false information through all available media to its citizens—about how good their own country is and how bad the enemies are. This will create a psychological effect upon the minds of its citizens.

I read in the newspaper of how the North Korean government prints millions of booklets propagating that America and its allies are against them, and that is the reason North Korea needs to build its own nuclear weapons to protect her nation. Can you imagine what it would be like for an average citizen growing up under such a controlling environment where this kind of information is being fed daily into his or her mind?

This is what Satan is doing right now through his own psychological warfare. He is successfully spreading false and deceitful doctrines, which are crossing borders and infiltrating the Church.

The minds of our youths are held captive in so-called religious worship that appeals to their minds and their flesh, just like the seeds found in the stony ground in the parable of the sower. They welcome the Word, endure it for a while, but when trouble comes, they get offended and backslide (Mark 4:16–17).

1 TIMOTHY 4:1 NKJV

Now the Spirit expressly says that in latter times some will depart from the faith, giving heed to deceiving spirits and doctrines of demons.

Come back to Jesus, my friend. It will be an awful experience to be left behind in the rapture, when Jesus comes secretly for His watchful Church (1 Corinthians 15:52; 1 Thessalonians 4:16–17).

This is what you must do now—cast off all of the backslidden reasoning that pulled you away from the knowledge of God. Become captivated by the love of God again. Be delivered from being so full of yourself.

2 CORINTHIANS 10:5 AMPC

[Inasmuch as we] refute arguments and theories and reasonings and every proud and lofty thing that sets itself up against the [true] knowledge of God; and we lead every thought and purpose away captive into the obedience of Christ (the Messiah, the Anointed One).

BE WATCHFUL IN PRAYER

The word *watch* comes from the Greek word *phulake*, meaning "to guard and to be spiritually alert" (Acts 20:31; 1 Corinthians 16:13; Colossians 4:2; 1 Thessalonians 5:6, 10).

Fellow soldier, you need to pray that God will open your eyes to see the realm of the supernatural (Ephesians 1:17). This supernatural eyesight will give you a glimpse into the realm of the supernatural—into both worlds: the realm of heaven and the activity of the demonic kingdom.

This supernatural eyesight is granted to the child of God who desires to be used by the Lord. The only way to develop this ability to see in the realm of the spirit is to increase the time spent in prayer. However, it is through the will of the Lord that we can gain access into the realm of the spirit and not through clocking hours in prayer. Our relationship with God should be a holistic process of discipleship and godliness and is not based on chants and formulas of prayer, as some teach.

ROMANS 12:11

Never be lacking in zeal, but keep your spiritual fervor, serving the Lord.

2 TIMOTHY 1:6–7

For this reason I remind you to fan into flame the gift of God, which is in you through the laying on of my hands.

For God did not give us a spirit of timidity, but a spirit of power, of love and of self-discipline.

Prayer builds fervency in your spirit. The word *fervent* comes from the Greek word *zeo*, meaning "to be hot and to boil." That is exactly what happens when you become fervent in prayer. The spirit of fervency fans into flames the anointing of the Holy Spirit within. The gifts that God has placed in your life will be activated. You will become spiritually sensitive. The fear of man and the need for man's approval will leave you. The Spirit of power will take control of your life. The love you have for God and for people will increase as you become more self-disciplined in your walk with God. You will have a new burden for the passion for lost souls.

Become so hot for Jesus that the next time the devil touches you, he will get his hands burned! The fire of the glory of God is greater than the fires of hell! Hallelujah!

OPS BRIEFING 2

THE SPECIAL FORCE

The nation of Israel was slipping into its own dark ages. Her people were under oppression and fear. Many compromised their faith and allegiance to the God of Israel. Her kings were not walking right before the Lord. They were setting up altars for Baal worship. Many prophets were hiding, perhaps out of fear of dying at the hands of Jezebel. The Bible records that Jezebel was killing the Lord's prophets (1 Kings 18:4).

Perhaps some prophets cried to God before they died, "Lord! Send someone to avenge our blood!" The prophets hidden by Obadiah could have cried out to God, "Please send someone to deliver us, O Lord!"

"Elijah appeared in zero hour in Israel's history. Things could hardly have been worse. When wickedness develops into extraordinary proportions, God meets it with extraordinary measures. In this case, His method was a man, the rugged Elijah, whose appearance was as dramatic and volcanic as his nature. God is never at a loss for a man to match the hour. When the devil seems to have seized the initiative, God replies by producing His own champion, endowed with personality and gifts appropriate to the task. Jezebel challenged the existence of Jehovah. Elijah was the answer."[4]

Today, we are facing the same kind of spiritual disease working itself through the Church. Many (not all) servants of God are given to the flattery of glamorized Christianity; they are exchanging the altars of the Lord for tables of business (Matthew 21:12). The anointing is being merchandised.

Our Lord Jesus bled through Calvary to release the pure oil from heaven, while these ministers smile with greed and release alternative oil from their souls.[5] The voices of these mixed breeds of ministers are better heard as they speak what people want to hear rather than the word of the Lord.

Because the Church has been "successful" in fighting off the true prophets of the Lord who come from the presence of God, Satan releases the "alternative" prophets, who are wolves in sheep's clothing (Matthew 7:15). They come to plunder the work and the resources of the house of the Lord, out of their own selfish motives. Their mouths speak lies and messages of falsehood (2 Peter 2:3).

Pastors, I urge you in the name of Jesus—get back to the altar of prayer so that you will know whom the Lord is sending to your church. Ask the Lord to open your eyes of the spirit (Ephesians 1:18) to know the difference between a true prophet and a false

---

4 J. Oswald Sanders, *Men Who Met God* (London: Marshall, Morgan & Scott, 1980), 119.

5 Steven Francis, *Fragrance Plus Anointing* (Rivers of Life Visions International, 2003).

one. Do not be afraid of the Lord's rebuke or correction through His prophets. They are sent by the Lord to help you build the house of the Lord (Ezra 5:2), not "your" church. The Lord may send a prophet hidden (1 Kings 19:18) in His hand (Isaiah 49:16) to minister the word of the Lord to your congregation. He or she may not be known to the Church at large, but they will be known and approved by God (2 Corinthians 10:18; 2 Timothy 2:15).

For the Lord says, "For many of My servants are in the making through My pruning hands. They are purged through the fire of My Spirit. My eyes are watching their every move. I will lead them to the right places, to the right churches, to bear forth My Word."[6]

THE COMPANY OF THE SEVEN THOUSAND

As the anointing of the Lord filled me in the church, the Holy Spirit brought an outburst of revelation into my spirit. My heart prayed, "God, release the company of the seven thousand!" I remembered the Scripture from 1 Kings 19. As I pondered, the Lord taught me instantly. I desire to inspire and teach you that which the Lord has taught me through the Spirit of revelation and the Word of God.

The number "seven thousand" symbolizes completeness and divinity. The Bible mentions, "I have reserved seven thousand **in Israel.**" This is a very clear statement that, at the time of its saying, was possibly a figure of speech. What about those of us who are not from Israel, the Gentiles?

---

6 Kuala Lumpur International Airport, Malaysia. August 31, 2005, 1943 hrs.

In the New Covenant, the Apostle Paul, through the inspiration of the Holy Spirit, wrote in Galatians 3:26–29, "For in Christ Jesus you are all sons of God through faith. For as many [of you] as were baptized into Christ [into a spiritual union and communion with Christ, the Anointed one, the Messiah] have put on (clothed yourselves with) Christ. There is [now no distinction] neither Jew nor Greek, there is neither slave nor free, there is not male and female; for you are all one in Christ Jesus. And if you belong to Christ [are in Him Who is Abraham's Seed], then you are Abraham's offspring and [spiritual] heirs according to promise" (AMPC).

ROMANS 2:29 AMPC

But he is a Jew who is one inwardly, and [true] circumcision is of the heart, a spiritual and not a literal [matter]. His praise is not from men but from God.

In this Church Age, we are all Abraham's offspring and heirs according to God's promise. The covenants and blessings that the Lord made with the Israelites and promised to them apply to us, as well. We are God's covenant people, the apple of His eye (Deuteronomy 32:10; Psalm 17:8; Zechariah 2:8).

THE SECOND COMING OF JESUS

The Holy Spirit highlighted this equation: seven multiplied by one thousand equals seven thousand. These numbers, seven and one thousand, are important figures in the book of Revelation.

The number seven appears fifty-four times in the book of Revelation. Some passages that use the number seven relating to God, His works, and angels include:

- Revelation 1:4: Seven churches
- Revelation 1:4: Seven spirits who are on His throne
- Revelation 1:12: Seven golden lampstands
- Revelation 1:16: Seven stars in His right hand
- Revelation 4:5: Seven lamps of fire
- Revelation 5:1: Seven seals (Revelation 6:1–8:5)
- Revelation 5:6: Seven horns and seven eyes
- Revelation 8:2: Seven angels and seven trumpets (Revelation 8:7–11:19)
- Revelation 10:3: Seven thunders
- Revelation 15:1: Seven plagues (Revelation 16:21)
- Revelation 15:7: Seven golden bowls full of the wrath of God

The number "one thousand," on the other hand, appears in Revelation 20:2, where Satan will be bound for a thousand years, and in Revelation 20:5, the Bible speaks of the thousand-year reign of Christ on the earth.

As the Second Coming of Jesus draws nigh, I believe the captain of the Lord of Hosts is gathering His army for the end-time battle. The Church will rise in such a power like the world has never seen before. There will be an awesome anointing of the Lord Jesus coming upon His Church, such that those who scorn, mock, and swear at the name of Jesus will be touched by the miraculous power of God.

We will witness a strong outpouring of the Holy Spirit coming upon the nations of the world like waves of the ocean, resulting in countless numbers of souls being saved by the power of God. The tsunami that the world witnessed on December 26, 2004, took hundreds of thousands of lives, but the power of the Holy Spirit that is coming is greater even than that tsunami, and it will result in millions of souls being saved.

The Lord told Elijah, "I have reserved"—this reservation is the work of the Lord Himself. We are to prepare ourselves for the selection process of Jesus, choosing those who are to join this special force company. As we are faithful in each phase and each level of ministry, the Lord promotes us to greater heights in Him and for Him.

People will be chosen according to the predetermined will of the Father and through the faithful surrender and obedience seen in the lives of the eager children of God (Ephesians 1:4; 2 Timothy 1:9). It needs to be emphasized again that when I use the phrase "special force," I am not referring to the Church at large, but rather to the individuals whom God selects for important tasks.

In these present times, God is training up a remnant, which I believe is being kept hidden by Him for the end times. This company of specially trained warriors will be mightily used by the Lord to bring the Church, her ministers, and God's people into divine alignment with the will of the Father. Their ministries will shine as a glorious light during that period when seeming darkness will fall upon the face of the earth and take over for some time. (This is the period of the rule of the Antichrist.)

This company, chosen by the grace of God and their faithfulness in the Lord's works, will be trained in the "Old Testament ways" of wilderness training in the school of the Spirit. I am not implying that formal training in a Bible school is not important. However, each of us is responsible for carefully selecting the right school that imparts the Word and disciples us in God's ways. Through the training of both the Word and the Spirit, these end-time servants will have gained maturity in their spiritual lives, and they will possess the knowledge of the ways of God.

This company will have the Lord's signature upon their lives, as it consists of men and women who are designed, made, and produced by the Lord. When you see them, you will know that this company is nevertheless "made and fashioned" by the hand of the Lord (Psalm 119:73; 139:14; Job 10:8; Isaiah 64:8). The growing stages of their natural lives, the seasons in which they enter, and the coordinates of their spiritual training are all preordained for them by the Commander-in-Chief Himself (Psalm 139:16). The Bible says this in Acts 4:13: "When they saw the courage of Peter and John and realized that they were unschooled, ordinary men, they were astonished and they took note that these men had been with Jesus."

I am neither promoting nor advocating elitism in the Body of Christ, but I am simply stating that each one is called according to the grace of God. Some will be chosen to be in the fivefold ministry, while others are called to stand in their call as witnesses of the Lord Jesus.

In 1 Corinthians 12:29–30, Paul wrote, "Are all apostles? Are all prophets? Are all teachers? Do all work miracles? Do all have gifts of healing? Do all speak in tongues? Do all interpret?" The answer is, "It was he who gave some to be apostles, some to be prophets, some to be evangelists, and some to be pastors and teachers" (Ephesians 4:11).

YOU ARE NOT THE ONLY ONE, MATE!

1 KINGS 19:18 NKJV

Yet I have reserved seven thousand in Israel, all whose knees have not bowed to Baal, and every mouth that has not kissed him.

Brethren, don't let the devil or your mind trick you into thinking that you are the only one who is going through any particular problem at any given moment, or you are the only one whose church or ministry is obedient to fulfill the perfect will of God.

Satan tries his best to bring such an onslaught against the people of God, inducing them to harbor thoughts of self-pity: *I feel so sorry for myself.* Once these thoughts are accepted and meditated upon, they will release the spirit of discouragement and despair. As manipulative and seductive as the devil can be, he will twist your thoughts and project his mind onto you, either to build up the self-pity spirit or the spirit of self-pride, which thinks, *I am the only one standing, and everyone else is unfaithful.*

When I was sixteen years old, the enemy tempted me to think such thoughts of pride and self-righteousness. Every morning I would wake up at 4 a.m. and spend two hours in prayer before going to school. It was difficult, but the joy and anticipation of speaking to Jesus overtook my lazy flesh.

One morning when I woke up at four, and as I was brushing my teeth, I heard a voice, *There are not many youths like you who will wake up early in the morning just to pray. While others are enjoying their beds, you are awake to seek God.* While these words were projected on my mind, I did not think anything of it. But then, before I could think otherwise, there was another voice that rose up in authority and spoke, *Yes, but at sixteen years old Sadhu Sundar Singh*[7] *was out preaching and serving God. He was poisoned by his father and left to die for the sake of Jesus. You are just here in your nice room praying.*

The Lord has taught me and is still teaching me many lessons on how to shun the spirit of pride. You must discern the difference between the connection that comes from God and the connections that are inspired by the devil. At times, Satan will open alternative doors of ministry to tempt overzealous ministers. If they respond to such invitations, these servants will be in the wrong place with the wrong people.

The Apostle Paul had to be taught not to be overzealous in ministry, which only invited unnecessary opposition (Acts 9:23–25, 29-30). Paul had to learn from the Lord that all ministry

---

[7] Phyllis Thompson, *Sadhu Sundar Singh* (OM Publishing, 1992).

engagements that are of divine origin will hit the bull's-eye with maximum impact for the Kingdom of God (Romans 1:16; 1 Corinthians 2:4–5).

1 KINGS 19:3–5

Elijah was afraid and ran for his life. When he came to Beersheba in Judah, he left his servant there, while he himself went a day's journey into the desert. He came to a broom tree, sat down under it and prayed that he might die. "I have had enough, Lord," he said. "Take my life; I am no better than my ancestors." Then he lay down under the tree and fell asleep.

Perhaps Elijah grew up thinking that he must be as good as his forefathers were. He could have measured himself by the stories of the faithful men and women of God passed down through the oral tradition of the Hebrew culture. But when fear overtook the better part of him, he just wanted to die.

If Elijah had known through revelatory foresight how God wanted to take him away in a chariot of fire, do you think he would have spoken those words? Of course not! Any one of us would have endured "hell on earth" just to experience that glorious moment.

ONLY ONE WAY—GOD'S WAY!

In this school of the Spirit, you still must learn. Regardless of how mature you are in the Lord or how long you have served Him in the full-time ministry, you have the choice either to obey or to disobey the Lord. The longer you walk with Christ, the narrower the road becomes, not wider. Biblical and Church history confirms this pattern.

If you have not taken this course on the deeper walk in Christ, you will not understand how it is possible for senior and seasoned servants of God to fall. Some recover, and some do not.

How was it possible for Moses to disobey God by striking the rock twice (Numbers 20:8–12) when he was a man who spoke to God face-to-face (Exodus 33:11)? Why did Abraham lie to Abimelech, telling him that Sarah was his sister (Genesis 20:2), even though he knew God was with him? How was it possible for the children of Israel to disobey and doubt the power of God after having witnessed multiple demonstrations of the might of God, some of which have never been repeated in biblical history (Psalm 78:43–58)?

How is it possible for some present-day, contemporary ministers who have known God in intimate fellowship to fall away from the faith? If it was possible for them, it is possible for us to fall from grace if we are also careless in our spiritual walk.

My friends, no matter how close you are to God, there will always be a vast difference between man and God (Exodus 19:12; Joshua 3:4). You cannot, at any point in time, know all about God—not now nor even in eternity. The Bible says in Deuteronomy 29:29, "The secret things belong to the Lord our God, but the things revealed belong to us and to our children forever, that we may follow all the words of this law." No matter how close you get to God, remember to "take off your sandals; for the place where you are standing is holy ground" (Exodus 3:5).

You cannot let an attitude of familiarity denigrate your sacred relationship with God. Satan uses this weapon in our moments of weakness. It is just like how Satan subtly attacked Samson: "He awoke from his sleep and thought, 'I'll go out as before and shake myself free.' But he did not know that the Lord had left him" (Judges 16:20).

As we are human, the possibility for us to make errors and misjudge the seasons and the timings will always be there. That is the reason each one of us must consistently maintain a spirit of prayer and repentance (1 Corinthians 8:9; 10:12; Colossians 4:17; Hebrews 3:12).

MANY ARE CHOSEN; FEW ARE CALLED

The Bible says that not all are called into the fivefold ministry. If all are in the fivefold ministry, then who will the believers be who is to build up the Church? If all are commanders, then who are the foot soldiers? In the early 1980s, when the Holy Spirit released a revelation of understanding of the fivefold ministry, many churches began identifying each one of their believers as one of the fivefold ministers. This misinformation and error in understanding brought about great confusion, pride, and prejudice in the churches. Many believers in these churches (although not all) called themselves to be someone with a calling to the fivefold ministry, and they walked around in pride with an unteachable spirit.

History is largely the tale of God using ordinary people to accomplish His extraordinary purposes throughout time.[8] Brian Edwards concluded: "The point is that God has almost always used particular men to lead His work. That is His method."[9]

God has always chosen individuals to walk the extra mile of faith and obedience to fulfill God's specific will (Hebrews 11), people such as Enoch, Abraham, Joseph, Moses, Deborah, Esther, Ruth, Naomi, Samuel, Isaiah, Jeremiah, and Ezekiel, just to name a few.

However, the Lord always calls individuals to serve Him in an increased capacity, such as serving in a full-time ministry. These men and women are called to forsake the world and her promises and instead follow the Master and fulfill His will for their lives. These "called-out ones" take the faith journey seriously and go wherever the Lord leads them, according to their individual callings (Ephesians 4:11).

Henry Blackaby wrote, "God isn't interested in merely giving you a mission's experience, but in your being on mission with Him. God reveals Himself to you so you can adjust your life to Him and join Him on His mission. Where He takes you is His doing, not yours. He wants to reveal His glory to a waiting world through you. He can do that anywhere He chooses when you allow Him to manifest Himself through you. As you experience God on

---

8 Henry Blackaby, and Richard Blackaby, *Called to be God's Leader* (Nashville, Tenn.: Thomas Nelson, 2004), ix.

9 Brian Edwards, *Revival! A People Saturated with God* (Darlington, England: Evangelical Press, 1990; reprint ed., 1994), 47.

mission, you do not choose your experiences, your assignment, or your location, He does. Your ultimate goal is to allow God to reveal Himself to you and then through you to others."[10]

The compelling question is: Why does God use some people for His purposes and not others? Does God not want His Kingdom to expand in every place and in every age? Does He not intend for His will to be done on earth as it is in heaven? With so many people worldwide claiming to be Christ's followers, why does God not work mightily through each one? Would not such an overwhelming outpouring of God's power cause every knee to bow and every tongue to confess Jesus as Lord? Yet God does not work that way. He is selective in those He uses. When God places His hand upon a life, the effect is unmistakable. But many Christians today show little evidence of God's presence in their lives; consequently, they fail to make a significant difference for God's Kingdom. They live their lives without impacting their world.[11] God continues to work through those who are willing to pay the necessary price to walk with Him.[12]

God calls everyone, but not everyone has the desire to pay the price to press on into the high calling of Jesus Christ (Philippians 3:14). All, however, are called to play an important supportive role in the Body of Christ, which is just as important as being a member of the fivefold ministry. The issue is not about your name

---

10 Avery T. Willis Jr., and Henry T. Blackaby, *Experiencing God* (Nashville, Tenn.: Broadman & Holman Publishers, 2002), 3.

11 Henry Blackaby, Richard Blackaby, *Called to Be God's Leader* (Nashville, Tenn.: Thomas Nelson Publishers, 2004), ix

12 Ibid., xi.

tag telling who you are, but rather it is about obedience to the purposes of God for your life.

GALATIANS 3:26

You are all sons of God through faith in Christ Jesus.

1 CORINTHIANS 12:12, 14–27 THE MESSAGE

You can easily enough see how this kind of thing works by looking no further than your own body. Your body has many parts—limbs, organs, cells—but no matter how many parts you can name, you're still one body. It's exactly the same with Christ. I want you to think about how all this makes you more significant, not less. A body isn't just a single part blown up into something huge. It's all the different-but-similar parts arranged and functioning together.

If Foot said, "I'm not elegant like Hand, embellished with rings; I guess I don't belong to this body," would that make it so? If Ear said, "I'm not beautiful like Eye, transparent and expressive; I don't deserve a place on the head," would you want to remove it from the body? If the body was all eye, how could it hear? If all ear, how could it smell? As it is, we see that God has carefully placed each part of the body right where he wanted it. But I also want you to think about how this keeps your significance from getting blown up into self-importance. For no matter how significant you are, it is only because of what you are a part of. An enormous eye or a gigantic hand wouldn't be a body, but a monster.

> *What we have is one body with many parts, each its proper size and in its proper place. No part is important on its own. Can you imagine Eye telling Hand, "Get lost; I don't need you"? Or, Head telling Foot, "You're fired; your job has been phased out"? As a matter of fact, in practice it works the other way—the "lower" the part, the more basic, and therefore necessary. You can live without an eye, for instance, but not without a stomach. When it's a part of your own body you are concerned with, it makes no difference whether the part is visible or clothed, higher or lower. You give it dignity and honor just as it is, without comparisons. If anything, you have more concern for the lower parts than the higher. If you had to choose, wouldn't you prefer good digestion to full-bodied hair?*
>
> *The way God designed our bodies is a model for understanding our lives together as a church: every part dependent on every other part, the parts we mention and the parts we don't, the parts we see and the parts we don't. If one part hurts, every other part is involved in the hurt, and in the healing. If one part flourishes, every other part enters into the exuberance. You are Christ's body—that's who you are! You must never forget this. Only as you accept your part of that body does your "part" mean anything.*

There is much repentance needed in the Body of Christ, as we are tempted to elevate ourselves to show the importance of our ministries and the accuracy of our messages above others. The

Bible says we are all doing the part that God designed us to do. May God help us!

If you are "not selected" to join this special force (to be in one of the fivefold ministries), you are to continue serving the will of the Father in other various ministries (Romans 12:6; Ephesians 4:7; Mark 16:15–18; Luke 10:19) to preach the salvation to the lost, to build and serve faithfully in the Church. Make yourself an asset to the Church and not a liability!

THE STRATEGY OF THE CHURCH, TOTAL DEFENSE SYSTEM

The Church of Jesus Christ must seriously rethink her strategies to prevail against the gates of hell, press forward against the invasion of the spirit of the world, and renew the passion of her people to fight for the cause of Jesus Christ. Jesus commanded His Church to prevail, not blend in.

Satan's power has not increased; Christ's Church has simply failed in large numbers to take her role seriously. Believers have left the field of battle in droves. Our view of ourselves as soldiers has become passé, diminished, or disregarded. In fact, the gates of hades is prevailing almost unchallenged in the lost world. They must be confronted by believers who will live out their confession within the shadows, laying siege to the gates of hades. The cautious, disengaged Church is certainly no threat to the unseen authorities; in fact, she has become an aid and an ally to them by her silence and lethargy. The Church has a victim mentality, being unable or unwilling to take the offensive. The world is waiting, and the gates of hades are daring the Church to be the Church![13]

Like an automobile, most churches are equipped with a "rearview mirror." Believers often spend more time looking at where they came from rather than at where they're going.[14] We need to honor the past revivalists and ministries of how God used them. We should learn from them. We should not, however, idolize their personalities or accomplishments, which were done by the enablement of the Holy Spirit, to a degree that brings an inferiority feeling in us. We can be on the lookout for their weaknesses so much that you can overlook your own weaknesses. In the Old Testament, we read of the heroes of faith, both men and women who lived outstanding lives for God and demonstrated an admirable faith. In the New Testament, the Apostle Paul focuses on "you," the Church. You can do all things in Christ by the power of the Holy Spirit living in you.

For believers to develop a mentality of living for the cause of God, there is a need for a holistic approach to disciple-making rather than just majoring in the power dynamics of church growth.

SINGAPORE'S TOTAL DEFENSE STRATEGY

I was reminded of Singapore's Total Defense Strategy, implemented in 1984. The write-up from the government's official

---

13 Randy Pope, *The Prevailing Church* (Chicago: Moody Press, 2002), 31.

14 Stan Toler, Glen Martin, *Survival Skills* (Kansas City, Miss.: Beacon Hill Press, 2002), 17.

website gives us a greater understanding of this strategy.[15] As a young nation with a small population, Singapore could not afford to maintain an armed forces on a regular basis. Thus, there was the need to involve every Singaporean to multiply the nation's defense capability.

Second, the nature of modern warfare has changed. Wars are no longer limited to the physical battlefield. Instead, aggressors can strike in less obvious, nonmilitary ways. This Total Defense Strategy provided the framework for a comprehensive and integrated response to deal with all kinds of threats and challenges.

Likewise, our Lord Jesus has given us the fivefold defense system (Ephesians 4:11–15) to build the Church from within and to protect the Church from without.

THE SUPER-APOSTLE SYNDROME

Each of the fivefold ministries carries an aspect of the ministry of the Triune God. Each ministry has its own peak seasons in the duration of its service. The fivefold ministries as a whole are as active now as they ever were to usher in the Second Coming of Jesus Christ. The fivefold ministries are called into a governmental anointing to bring growth and order to the Body of Christ.

Who is important in the fivefold ministry? Our Lord Jesus is. The rule of Jesus is simple and direct. He who is the greatest must be the servant of all (Matthew 18:4; 23:11). There are no super-apostles of any kind in any part of the world (2 Corinthians 10:12). Each

---

[15] http://www.totaldefence.org.sg.

of us is to be faithful according to the given task (Romans 12:3; 1 Corinthians 4:2). I heard one "super-apostle" saying in a video sermon that he downloads his revelation from God and everyone else is just copying after him. Another guy I heard was called the "Patriarch Apostle." Then you have those who give "apostle ordination" so that they can tithe to the super apostle.

In these present days, we are hearing of many preachers saying they are the "super-apostles," called to teach the Body of Christ and change the world. I am sad, not only for these men, but also for their followers; they have no time to seek the Lord, as they are engulfed in these false doctrines of men. These ministers "conform to an appearance of spirituality but live out of a wrong spirit."[16]

"When we build reputations that are not based on the character of Christ, but on the imitation of a ministry model or style or an image of success, popularity or perhaps spirituality, then the lie must be maintained, resulting in deep spiritual dissonance. We experience a lack of inner harmony with God and with others, making it very difficult to be real and vulnerable."[17]

THE END-TIME RESTORATION OF THE FIVEFOLD MINISTRY

We are going to witness the restoration and the united force of the fivefold ministries in their totality. All these men and women will sign off their ministries with the message of the Second

[16] David Orton, *Snakes in the Temple* (Kent, England: Sovereign World, 2004), 70.

[17] Ibid., 75.

Coming of Jesus and prepare the Body of Christ to appear before Him (2 Corinthians 5:10–11).

There are many books about the fivefold ministry. I recommend the reading of *He Gave Gifts Unto Men* by Kenneth Hagin. I have given my understanding in brief of these callings and anointings.

1. Apostle: He carries the mind of the Lord. The big picture of the purposes of the Lord and the spiritual state of the nations of the world are his concerns. The apostle brings alignment to the Church by assisting in adopting changes in the structural systems of the Church. He establishes Kingdom-minded communities to enable believers to stand firm against the coming persecution of the last days (Acts 4:32–36).

2. Prophet: He carries the eye of the Lord. There will be schools of prophets, who will become watchmen of the cities. The Holy Spirit will enable them to see the coming moves of God and the onslaught of the enemy against churches and nations. These men and women will sound the trumpet. The might and fervency of the Lord will be imparted through the prophets to the Body of Christ to stand against the works of the enemy (Psalm 18:29).

3. Evangelist: He becomes the mouth of the Lord, speaking salvation to the nations. The message of the soon-coming return of Jesus will echo through the evangelists around the world again (Matthew 4:17). These servants will be anointed with the power of God, and signs and wonders will follow them in greater ways (Acts 5:5).

4. Pastor: He carries the heart of the Lord for His people (Ezekiel 34:11–16). The Church will grow in the Lord's wisdom and stature (Luke 2:52). A greater faith and obedience will mark the lives of the believers (Acts 2:42–47). The end-time Church will be a triumphant Church that overcomes the wiles of the enemy. The Church of the end times will walk in greater discernment (Isaiah 7:15).
5. Teacher: He carries the Word of the Lord to the Body of Christ. The spirit of wisdom and revelation will rest upon the teachers of the Word (Ephesians 1:17). The Church will experience the realm of the heavenlies through the teachings of the Word. Jesus Himself will become the Bread of Heaven and will draw His people to Himself (John 6:48, 51; 12:32; Ephesians 3:17).

Each of these callings will trumpet the Second Coming of Christ and prepare the Church to face the coming challenges.

The Lord Jesus is going to unleash the fiercest army that the world has ever seen, and Satan and his cohorts have no clue about it yet. The Church will not lose. We will win. We will overcome!

OPS BRIEFING 3

THE LANDMINES OF THE ENEMY

Some years ago, I was invited to speak at a pastors and leaders seminar in Cambodia. I was so grief-stricken by the condition of this war-torn country. There was so much pain and resentment in the hearts of the people against one another. What shocked me further were the hundreds of people I saw on the streets begging. A large percentage of them, both young and old, had only one leg. I came to understand that they were victims of landmines.

"Landmines—laid by the Khmer Rouge, the Heng Samrin, and Hun Sen regimes, the Vietnamese, the KPNLF, and the Sihanoukists—litter the countryside. In most cases, even the soldiers who planted the mines did not record where they were placed. Now, Cambodia has one of the highest rates of physical disability of any country in the world. While census data for Cambodia is sketchy, it is generally accepted that more than 40,000 Cambodians have suffered amputations as a result of mine injuries since 1979."[18]

[18] http://www.mekong.net/cambodia/mines.htm.

One of the deadliest legacies of the twentieth century is the use of landmines in warfare. Anti-personnel landmines continue to have tragic, unintended consequences years after a battle and even after the entire war has ended. As time passes, the locations of landmines are often forgotten, even by those who planted them.

These mines continue to be functional for many decades, causing further damage, injury, and death to innocent civilians.

Landmines are devices that have been designed to explode when triggered by pressure or a tripwire. These devices are typically found on or just below the surface of the ground. The purpose of these mines, when used by armed forces, is to disable any person or vehicle that comes in contact with it through an explosion or fragments released at high speeds. Landmines are intended to produce an obstacle effect on an enemy's maneuvers and reduce their options for courses of action when they attack.

Currently, there are more than 100 million landmines located in seventy countries around the world, according to OneWorld International. Since 1975, landmines have killed or maimed more than one million people, which has led to a worldwide effort to ban further landmine use and clear away existing landmines.[19]

IN THE REALM OF THE SPIRIT WORLD

One of the physical injuries caused by landmines of a lesser degree is the dismemberment of the legs of the victim. As a result,

---

[19] http://science.howstuffworks.com/landmine.htm.

the victim usually must undergo surgery to amputate the injured leg in order to save his or her life.

Our enemy, Satan, has set many landmines intended to cause setbacks to the overall progress of believers and the Church. That is why we need to learn to walk in the Spirit and adhere to the counsel of God through His Word. God will send prophets that can detect demonic presence and activity in each region that is causing problems for the Church. The only plan Satan has is to stop or slow down the believers' walk in Christ.

The enemy may lull us into a sense of false immunity. Often mild temptations, when successfully resisted, deceive us about our moral strength. Then Satan turns his big guns upon our unguarded flanks, right where we thought we were so strong! Guard your "strong" points. We can despise those who fall, which is a way of drawing attention to our own superior holiness. Never underestimate satanic subtlety. Only the saving grace of Jesus preserves our feet from slipping.[20]

WALK WORTHILY FOR CHRIST

EPHESIANS 4:1 AMPC

I, therefore, the prisoner for the Lord, appeal to and beg you to walk (lead a life) worthy of the [divine] calling to which you have been called [with behavior that is a credit to the summons to God's service.

[20] Reinhard Bonnke, *Evangelism by Fire* (Full Flame GmbH, 2001), 265.

Don't let the enemy interfere with your walk in Christ. The Apostle Paul, through the Holy Spirit, issued a higher standard of living for those who are called by the Lord. If we will be fervent to walk in the Spirit, then we will not fulfill the lust of the flesh (Galatians 5:16). It is not enough just to know the Word and its doctrines; we must also walk in the Spirit in obedience to the Scriptures.

1 TIMOTHY 4:15–16

Be diligent in these matters; give yourself wholly to them, so that everyone may see your progress.

Watch your life and doctrine closely. Persevere in them, because if you do, you will save both yourself and your hearers.

We must pay close attention to the conduct of our lives and the formulation and understanding of the doctrines of Christ. It must be built upon and rooted in the Word of God. The Bible warns us to:

EPHESIANS 5:15–16 AMPC

Look carefully then how you walk! Live purposefully and worthily and accurately, not as the unwise and witless, but as wise (sensible, intelligent people).

Making the very most of the time [buying up each opportunity], because the days are evil.

Many soldiers in the Lord's camp are walking around with broken legs. Some of them are victims of church abuse, some are victims of manipulative and controlling leadership, and some are victims through their own doing and are suffering the consequences of disobedience.

BE HEALED IN YOUR WALK

Fellow soldier, stop behaving like a "war veteran" in the Church by always saying, "Been there, done that!" The army of God needs you. Come back from your "flesh retirement" and join the school of the Holy Spirit again. There is no "retirement" in the spirit for a warrior. The *R*s in your life are *Revival, Resurrection, Retrain, Revisit,* and *Relaunch*!

I prophesy to you through the authority of God's Word and His anointing vested on me, if you are willing to set your heart right before the Lord—if you would repent from your ways and be willing to be obedient to the ways of God—the same Jesus who healed the sick and made the lame to walk again (Matthew 11:5) will heal you from your spiritual paralysis and lameness.

You could have suffered spiritual broken legs until you had no more confidence to do what God wants you to do. Instead, I speak the creative power of God over your life and into your spirit. I command this soul bondage you are under to be broken in Jesus' name. Walk again in His name and believe from now on for a new boldness in the Spirit, a new courage to be what God wants you to be. Walk wisely, avoiding all familiar landmines. Help others avoid them. Be a lifesaver of your brethren in the Body of Christ.

THE SNARE OF THE TRAPPER

PSALM 91:3 NASB

For it is He who delivers you from the snare of the trapper and from the deadly pestilence.

The enemy of our souls is always busy trying to weaken the position of the child of God by setting snares and traps for him. He is afraid of your anointing, the calling, prayer life, time of meditation of the Word, and boldness in the Spirit. The Bible says that God sets us free from the snare of the trapper. Hallelujah!

The Bible teaches us how to recognize the snares and traps of the enemy and how to avoid them. The army of the Lord must learn both offensive and defensive strategies in this end-time war, to set the captives free and build the house of God.

Years ago, there were some teachings that were circulating about how believers could blackmail the devil by using their faith. Such teaching is a direct violation of the Scriptures, as the Bible says we are to engage the enemy from a position of victory and triumph (Romans 8:37; 1 Corinthians 15:57; 2 Corinthians 2:14).

COLOSSIANS 2:15 AMPC

[God] disarmed the principalities and powers that were ranged against us and made a bold display and public example of them, in triumphing over them in Him and in it [the cross].

My friend, there are no negotiations with the enemy. Satan has lost all his executive power over the righteous. He is trying to fool us into thinking he has some power left. The only door of access he has into our lives is by tempting us to sin and walk in disobedience. From that position of weakness and vulnerability, he launches his attacks. That's why sin steals the strength of the spirit. Sin steals the joy of the Lord from our hearts. Sin cancels your password to access the anointing of the Holy Spirit. Once Satan knows we are weak, he gains entry.

Beloved, the Chief Commander of the Lord of Hosts, Jesus Christ, has decreed that not one soldier must be left behind on the battlefield. You are on call for active duty. Get yourself washed in the blood of Jesus. Get back to your duty!

I want to specifically address the champions of Jesus who are being trained by the Spirit of God. The enemy will set many snares to trap your anointing and cause you to miscarry your destiny in Christ. I am speaking right at your spirit man: Enough of the "playing the victim" syndrome; enough of running away from your calling because you believe it is too hard. Stand up and face the works of the enemy with the wisdom of the Lord. When the Lord reveals Satan's attacks against you, learn to stand in the Spirit boldly.

The Lord, by the abundance of His grace toward me, has revealed the traps of the enemy against my family, against my ministry, against my fellow servants of God, against the churches I was pastoring, and against my physical safety. These warnings have come from other prophets and from the Lord Himself while I was waiting upon Him in prayer.

I want to admonish you prophetically through the Scriptures with some of these warnings.

LANDMINE # 1 THE FEAR OF MAN

PROVERBS 29:25 NKJV

The fear of man brings a snare, but whoever trusts in the LORD *shall be safe.*

The religious leaders tried hard to trap Jesus through His words and His ministry. The Bible says, "Then the Pharisees went and plotted how they might entangle Him in His talk" (Matthew 22:15 NKJV). Jesus always knew through the Spirit of revelation what their evil intent was, and He replied with the wisdom of God (Matthew 22:18).

The spirit of Jezebel will stir the religious leaders to fight against your boldness and the courage of your spirit if you so decide to walk as a radical for Jesus. In the name of brotherly unity, many prophets have kept their mouths shut from speaking out the voice of the Lord. Why is this so? The fear of man is the answer. Listen to me from your heart. I am neither advocating nor promoting rebellion in the Church, nor am I a supporter of church-hoppers or people with false, self-made visions.

The spirit of the fear of man hides under the cloaks of respect for elders, false unity, soulish bonds, the need to earn the appreciation of others, and many others. This spirit will instill fear inside your heart, in order to steal away your boldness and your courage in the Spirit. It may come in the form of threats against your future ministry success or invitations to preach in other churches.

Dear prophets and itinerant friends in the vineyard, if you choose to preach nice, cute little messages just to earn the favor of man or to receive more offerings, more contacts for meetings, ministry growth, and popularity instead of prophesying the Word of the Lord, the sword of the Lord will come against you, and your ministry will be shut down. Pleasers of men do not deserve to be the mouthpieces of the Lord Jesus.

Many immature and vulnerable prophets have lost their anointing and have compromised the Word of the Lord as their financial support dipped. Sadly, some have chosen to give out false prophecies and soulish visions in order to hype people up to receive big offerings. There is such a shaking in the prophetic community here in America that prophets are making public apologies in the media. The events of the world are beyond amateur prophets. Self-made prophets will suffer backlash. Immature prophets must learn to hold their tongue till God releases them to say matters in public. This lesson must be taught to the prophetic community—not everything that you hear in the secret place with God needs to be said out publicly. Some revelations are to be travailed in prayer only.

Some prophets and ministries, I noticed, are in a race to prophesy so that they could claim they were the first ones to prophesy it.

True prophets who walk with God will know when to be hidden and when to be public. Amid various world crises like Covid-19, may God filter through and reveal the true and mature prophets that His Church will be strong and united. May God reveal the flaky ones and expose them in Jesus Name.

In the month of January 2021, in an encounter with the Lord Jesus, I saw a vision of a big star falling from the sky. The Lord said, "A prominent minister will fall, then the judgment on other ministers will follow, including the prophetic community." Just as the Lord said, a world-renowned Christian minister died, many ministries were exposed, and there was a shaking in the prophetic community.

JEREMIAH 14:14 AMPC

Then the Lord said to me, The [false] prophets prophesy lies in My name. I sent them not, neither have I commanded them, nor have I spoken to them. They prophesy to you a false or pretended vision, a worthless divination [conjuring or practicing magic, trying to call forth the responses supposed to be given by idols], and the deceit of their own minds.

My pastor friends, I urge you to be mature in the Spirit and remain open to the work of the Holy Spirit. Rule your church with godly authority given by the Lord. Remember that you are God's servant given to the people and not the people's servant given to the Lord. Have a discerning heart to welcome those prophets sent by the Lord. Don't try to manipulate prophets to speak your messages or speak what you approve of. Don't entice prophets with bigger love offerings to speak nice messages to tickle the ears of your congregation (2 Timothy 4:3).

JEREMIAH 5:31 AMPC

The prophets prophesy falsely, and the priests exercise rule at their own hands and by means of the prophets. And My people love to have it so! But what will you do when the end comes?

Mark my words as His prophet, in these end times the Lord will cause you and your ministry to incur embarrassment if you continue to serve in the flesh. Such ministries that do not walk in the true anointing of the Lord are operating in false anointing and familiar spirits. Your ministry will be without effect in the Kingdom of God and will cause no damage to the kingdom of darkness. You will then become a parable, someone whom the Lord will use to warn other churches and ministers.

JEREMIAH 1:17 AMPC

But you [Jeremiah], gird up your loins! Arise and tell them all that I command you. Do not be dismayed and break down at the sight of their faces, lest I confound you before them and permit you to be overcome.

The Lord revealed to me that in these last days, we would witness the rise of strong contentions between the true and false prophets within the Church. One will be saying the true Word of the Lord, and the other will be saying the exact opposite to please the leader. The Lord Jesus is pouring the anointing of Jeremiah into the Church. The Lord Jesus will place the anointing of Jeremiah on selected individuals to speak as prophets to the Body of Christ. The Spirit of intercession and tears will become their benchmark, and they shall be burdened with passion for the Body of Christ. This breed of prophets will fight the false prophets, who are self-made and demon-sent within the Church.

Prophets, be sealed by Christ! Worry not about what the world calls you. The commendation of our Lord Jesus is more important than other people's opinions. Conduct your ministry according to the proportion of grace made available to you (Romans 12:3). Don't try to change the world with your zealousness or give in to the desire to travel around the world. Stay in the will of God. Fulfill the Lord's purpose.

During a prayer session at the Jerusalem conference (2010) conducted by Sadhu Sundar Selvaraj, he mentioned that the Lord was sealing His servants. I was on my knees weeping as the presence of God overwhelmed me. My spiritual eyes were opened. I saw a mirror in front of me. I saw my reflection in the mirror, and I saw a seal of the cross on my forehead. It was a thick iron-cast seal, like a scar in the flesh.

Since then, I have seen the seal of God in many meetings over selected individuals, those who are called to serve the Lord in a full-time capacity, especially for these end times.

LANDMINE # 2
LUST FOR GAIN AND WEALTH

1 TIMOTHY 6:9–10 NKJV

But those who desire to be rich fall into temptation and a snare, and into many foolish and harmful lusts which drown men in destruction and perdition.

For the love of money is a root of all kinds of evil, for which some have strayed from the faith in their greediness, and pierced themselves through with many sorrows.

Another trap the enemy sets up is by sending forth the spirit of lust for gain and wealth. I am not talking about the God-kind of prosperity, which includes financial blessings. I am addressing a false kind of prosperity, which many people run and seek after. It is not wrong to prosper, but it is a sin to have greed and covetousness. There should be a delicate balance between godly prosperity and the world's methods of prosperity.[21]

Sometimes ministries are easily tempted to merchandise the anointing or speak highly of their own importance in that they believe they are walking "more accurately" than others. The enemy may tempt you to "package" the anointing of God in a "lunchbox" and give it to the people. Satan will give a false assurance of financial support if you keep walking in the track of false spirituality operating in a false anointing.

[21] This reference of prosperity is made to prophets in the full-time ministry and not to the marketplace business leaders.

Aim to dazzle others, and you will dim God's glory. Preach for personal admiration, and the people who come to see God will only see the preacher.[22] Those privileged to exercise the gifts of the Spirit must be especially careful. Show-offs will be shown up. Spiritual gifts are not Oscar awards to be put on display, won as trophies of performance. Don't decorate yourself ostentatiously with God's power tools. Don't design tiaras, necklaces, and rings from the spiritual gifts for your own adornment.[23]

Many end-time warriors are losing ground and fighting the wrong battles out of the will of God because the money on the "other side" seems to be better. In Numbers 22, Balaam was one man who was enticed by Balak, the king of Moab.

My fellow warriors, we are called to live a life of sacrifice, but that does not mean we will live in poverty. A prophet will be supernaturally provided for by God.

God's prophet is expected of God to trust Him for supernatural providence, unlike other offices. The life of a disciplined warrior will increase the cause and gains of the Kingdom. You must overcome the snare of greed. The moment you are caught by your feet, the wealth you have accumulated will become a snare to your ministry and to your soul. We read of many ministers who have fallen away due to the misappropriation of finances.

If you ignore this weak spot, the enemy will bring his financiers to buy the Word of the Lord from your mouth. You will no longer

---

22 Reinhard Bonnke, *Evangelism by Fire* (Full Flame GmbH, 2001), 268.

23 Ibid., 249.

be the Lord's prophet; you will become their personal fortune teller (Deuteronomy 18:10). Trust in the Lord's provision. Our God is generous. He will elevate you and bless you with abundance.

Satan has sent his financiers to buy out struggling prophets who have not developed a strong faith to trust God for supernatural providences. One of the qualities of a prophet is walking with God in the unknown. The prophet walks in a supernatural faith trusting God will provide for all that God has commanded him to do.

Once while I was preaching in a conference, the Lord took me into a supernatural encounter. I was brought to the tribulation times. I saw a group of the remnant hiding in a dense forest. People were living there without much to eat, as they could not buy supplies because they had not received the mark of the beast.

Then I saw numerous angels coming down from heaven with baskets of food. I saw many kinds of fruits. I knew I was seeing them as "spirit fruits." The moment the feet of the angels touched the earth, the "spirit fruits" translated into earthly fruits. The angels came to supply the remnant supernaturally. Amen!

Your faith is able to translate God's promises in the Word into natural realities when you walk with God. Walk in obedience to His will, and you will taste and see the Lord is good. In the same way, the Lord has shown me in divine encounters how it is possible to draw from the supernatural health of heaven and translate it into natural health and strength (Proverbs 3:1–3).

LANDMINE # 3
WALKING IN THE WRONG COUNSEL

PROVERBS 3:32 AMPC

For the perverse are an abomination [extremely disgusting and detestable] to the Lord; but His confidential communion and secret counsel are with the [uncompromisingly] righteous (those who are upright and in right standing with Him).

In 1 Samuel 28, we read of King Saul seeking the counsel of a medium, a woman who operated in witchcraft and familiar spirits. As the Lord did not answer Saul through dreams, the Urim, or the prophets, Saul went to seek counsel from a sorcerer.

You see, my friends, the absence of the Spirit of revelation brings about the presence of confusion. The enemy capitalizes on such moments when the people of God walk without godly and divine counsel for their lives. The moment the enemy perceives that a child of God is no longer under a spiritual covering, he or she becomes a prime target for satanic deception.

I have witnessed godly servants of God become teachers of false doctrines because of their lack of submission to godly counsel. And because many such good people have not learned to respond rightly to godly correction, or at times divine chastisement (Deuteronomy 8:5; Hebrews 12:6), in the right manner, they harbor resentment and bitterness against anything that is right. They fight against the Church, the doctrines of the Word, and the counsels of the godly. Their hearts then become the breeding ground for the spirit of Korah.

THE SPIRIT OF KORAH

In Numbers 16, we read of the rebellion that Korah led against Moses. From a spiritual point of view, we can see the attack of this spirit of rebellion against the God-ordained anointing.

Many churches and ministries have died prematurely because of wrong counsel. Many believers remain barren in spirit and face manifold troubles because of rebellion and the judgment of the Lord that comes upon them. Some ministers walked in wrong counsel as the senior ministers failed to show them the path of the Lord or rebuke them when they went off-line.

A rebellious spirit operates under a canvas for the spirit of witchcraft (1 Samuel 15:23). The enemy is always on the lookout for those with a natural tendency to rebel against authority. These men and women, though they know Jesus as their Lord and have the Holy Spirit dwelling within them, have not allowed the Word of God to mold their character into His image, and so their rebellious nature remains hidden and unexamined. Such people operate in the realm of sense knowledge and worldly reasoning, propelled by pride and recognition.

2 CORINTHIANS 10:5 AMPC

[Inasmuch as we] refute arguments and theories and reasonings and every proud and lofty thing that sets itself up against the [true] knowledge of God; and we lead every

thought and purpose away captive into the obedience of Christ (the Messiah, the Anointed One).

PASTOR HIT BY MACHETE

I have withheld telling of this occurrence, as people who are young in the faith might get the wrong impression. Due to the nature of the subject, however, it would be right for me to share with you here how God views rebellion.

In 1996, I was invited by a pastor in Malaysia to minister in his church. Usually, after preaching, I would minister to hundreds of people. This prophetic time of prayer usually starts at about nine in the evening and will last until one in the morning.

When I prophesy over the people, I usually invite the senior pastor of the church or an elder to stand with me as a form of accountability. On this occasion, too, the senior pastor stood beside me. On this night, more than a hundred people lined up for prayer.

One brother named Jay (not his real name) came forward for prayer. However, as I laid my hands on his chest, I felt the anger of the Lord rising within me. I brought him aside from the crowd to speak in private with the senior pastor standing next to me. The Lord told me to tell Jay that if he would not repent from his ways, the judgment that was to come on him would also come on his family. After hearing these words, all of us shook with the fear of God.

One month later, Jay, who was only a few months old as a believer, wanted to be elected to the church board. During church services, he usually sat at the back of the church, and he would manipulate other church members with his own critical opinions about what the church should do.

One day, Jay threatened his senior pastor through criminal intimidation. Jay's former gang members showed up in the pastor's neighborhood. They rallied around the house in a truck in the middle of the night, carrying machetes and hurling verbal abuses against the pastor and his family. The pastor was embarrassed as the name of his church was put to shame. Some members of the church were so afraid they stopped going to church on Sundays.

The day of the church board elections came. The pastor stood his ground and appointed godly men and women to his church's council. Jay was so furious that he left right in the middle of the service. An hour later, just as the service was about to end, Jay and his gang members rushed back in through the front door of the church. As the pastor was still standing at the pulpit, Jay ran toward the front of the church, screaming, wielding a machete in his right hand. He took a swing at the pastor, but the pastor defended himself with his left arm and sustained a deep cut. Blood spurted all over the floor. Immediately, Jay and his gang left the church. The police were called in, and the pastor was rushed to the hospital. Thank God the slash was not deep. Although Jay and his gang were later arrested, the pastor decided to drop the charges against them.

Two weeks later, my phone rang at three in the morning. The caller was the pastor. I thought something bad must have happened for him to call me at such a late hour. He said, "Steven, you are a true prophet of God." "Why the early morning call?" I asked.

The pastor said, "Something has happened to Jay's family. Three nights ago, Jay and his wife left their eight-year-old daughter in their home and went to the nearby grocery store. Twenty minutes later, when they arrived back home, to their shock, their daughter laid motionless on the floor. They called an ambulance, and Jay's daughter was pronounced dead by the paramedics."

The pastor went on, "Jay called me to conduct the funeral service for his daughter. He fell at my feet and wept in repentance for all the things he had done to me and the church. I forgave him. Yesterday was the funeral. It was raining heavily. As the little coffin was lowered to the ground, the coffin began to float as water kept seeping in from the soil. At the sight of this, Jay's wife fell to the ground and cried out loudly, 'The soul of my daughter is not resting well!' The whole funeral service was a hard one. All the church people present knew that it was God's hand that had turned against Jay's family."

I felt the fear of God go down my spine. The Lord Jesus had offered Jay time to repent by revealing his sin and judgment. But like so many others, Jay did not think God was serious! I am writing this incident here in this book so that you will know how rebellion opens the door for the enemy to come in and harass both you and your family. Let us walk in unity and love in His Church for God's glory.

LANDMINE # 4
THE TEMPTATION OF THE FLESH

A couple of months ago, I received a phone call from a sister who had attended one of my meetings. She wanted to check with me about a particular leading from the Lord. She said that the Lord had told her to leave her husband and be united with one of her church pastors. Just then, my prophetic antennae went up. She continued, saying that she was to go through a spiritual transformation by living with this pastor for a year. She felt she was to separate herself from her family, the pastor was to leave his family, and they both were to stay together in their own household.

Without hesitation, I rebuked this sister. I told her that she had heard the voice of Satan and not the Lord. After a brief counseling session, she began to cry over the phone and repented.

How sad but alarming are the attacks of Satan against the people of God! This is exactly what the Lord revealed to me that Satan had launched an all-out attack against the purity of the Bride of Jesus.

The Lord revealed that Jezebel and her cohorts are actively planning to bring down ministers and split up their families. The increase of sex-oriented media that has produced a permissive culture is just one of the pieces of evidence of this spirit's dominance.

Sister Wendy Alec received a word when she experienced a divine visitation from the Lord.[24]

---

[24] Wendy Alec, *Journal of the Unknown Prophet* (Warboys Media, 2002), 275.

"My champions shall now know a violent satanic assailing against their minds. Any thought not taken captive shall be a thought that can take violent root in their souls to lead to ensnarement. Anything from their past that has been dealt with by their own strength and not by My Spirit shall become a snare to them and can leave them vulnerable to the enemy of their souls. Any habit not ruthlessly dealt with and put to the cross, when assigned with the searing heat of temptation, will breed and rapidly multiply."

Jesus continued speaking to her, "In this past age, Jezebel has translated itself into many different forms, but one of her primary forms, and one of her primary rules in this present age is her amalgamation with Babylon, the spirit of the world and lust—lust of the flesh, lust of the eyes, and the pride of life. Jezebel rules electronic media, film, television, and advertising—she is the epitome of seduction in this last age. She was Delilah, Salome, and Herodias. She rules over pornography, adultery, lasciviousness, homosexuality, pride, power, separation, divorce, ambition, and every perversion and sin of the flesh known to mankind. She tantalizes, packages sin, sells it, and then debases and exposes her victims before killing them. Her primary targets in this Church Age are My ministers, both men and women."

REVELATION 17:1–2

One of the seven angels who had the seven bowls came and said to me, "Come, I will show you the punishment of the great prostitute, who sits on many waters. With her the kings of the earth committed adultery and the inhabitants of the earth were intoxicated with the wine of her adulteries."

Satan is using the spirit of Jezebel as a feminine counterpart as he tries his best to stain the saints' garments of holiness and righteousness, thereby qualifying him to bring accusations against the servants of the Lord before the Father (Zechariah 3).

Most nations in the world have a problem with the sex industry.[25] The spirit of Jezebel defiles all cultures through uncleanness and fornication. The same spirit of defilement is attacking the people of God in the Church. Servants of God are not spared, either.

HOLINESS COMPROMISED IN THE HOUSE

Dr. Peter Wagner wrote that he once heard Cindy Jacobs say, "We can put on the whole armor of God, but if our hearts are not pure under it, we have holes in our armor!" In his book, he further wrote, "Satan and his principalities of darkness will be among the first to discover those holes, and we become extremely vulnerable to his fiery darts. The armor of God carries only a one-day warranty, so working on this needs to be a constant and daily part of our lifestyle."[26]

At times, Satan launches his attacks from within the Church. Some churches are fearful to establish moral dress codes for their church members during service times. Church leaders are afraid that if they do so, the members will see them as being legalistic. The standard for holiness has become so compromised that any

---

[25] http://www.catw-ap.org/facts.htm; http://www.icasa.org/uploads/prostitution.pdf; http://www.pucl.org/from-archives/Child/prostitution.htm.

[26] C. Peter Wagner, *Radical Holiness for Radical Living* (Colorado Springs, CO: Wagner Institute for Practical Ministry, 1998), 10.

distinguishing factor between the world and the Church seems very dim.

What happens when we dare to confront these issues? We allow the cleansing stream of the Holy Spirit to clean His house. We can then build a hedge of protection around the house of God. None of the members should ever become a tool in the hands of the enemy to cause the moral failure of another.

I want to include some excerpts of ministerial sexual problems for two purposes: one, to forewarn my fellow brethren, and second, to inform the general reader that ministers are human, too.

Let me quote from an article entitled "The Hidden Obsession," written by Harry W. Schaumburg and published in the *Enrichment Journal,* Fall 2005.[27] In Southeast Asia, the ministerial families are facing the same problems, with many falling away by moral failures and sexual misconduct. There is no statistical data to quote from. Nevertheless, we are to take heed to the counsel of our brethren:

"The tales of lust, sexual immorality, prostitution, homosexuality, sexual misconduct, addiction to pornography, and adultery should not be repeated. But to ignore the details causes further denial and spiritually corrodes the church. All too often those in authority are guilty of getting rid of the problem and moving on but fail to address the difficult issues that exist in the ministry. This is not the time or place to flinch at the external horror of our fallen brother or fail to examine the content of our own hearts."

---

27 Copyright ©2004 The General Council of the Assemblies of God. 1445 North Boonville Ave. Springfield, MO 65802-1894.

The Uncommon Stories

- Driven by lust and sexual fantasy, a pastor and his wife engaged in threesome sex with their twenty-year-old nanny. The pastor rationalized his behavior by citing the multiple wives of biblical characters.
- For years, a youth pastor corrupted his mind with sexual fantasies. He eventually had sexual relations with three underage girls and ultimately went to prison.
- A senior pastor became sexually involved with a married woman whom he was counseling. She became pregnant, and he paid for an abortion to cover his sin. Meanwhile, his wife gave birth to his child.
- A women's ministry pastor developed an emotional affair with a lay team leader. The two women eventually became sexually involved and refused to end their relationship, citing the importance of their spiritual and relational needs.
- A youth pastor was engaged in homosexual behavior with several young boys and ultimately committed suicide before he was arrested.
- An associate pastor who had been married for nineteen years had a seventeen-year affair with his secretary, who was his wife's best friend. For years, they vowed to God and to each other to end the relationship before it destroyed everyone in their lives, and yet they continued the relationship.
- A youth pastor's wife left her husband and two children to work in a strip club.

The Common Stories

The details are often repeated, but the pain, guilt, shame, and tears leave scars that will not disappear until Revelation 21:4 ESV is fulfilled: "He will wipe away every tear from their eyes, and death shall be no more, neither shall there be mourning nor crying nor pain anymore, for the former things have passed away."

The common stories include:

- The pastor who was caught with internet pornography on his office computer.
- The minister living in adultery that went undetected for months, even years.
- The missionary who drifted into various forms of sexual sin, visiting sex clubs, "legal" prostitution, and eventually sex with minors because it was easily available on the mission field.
- The pastor's wife who felt lonely and abandoned and found comfort in the arms of another man.

Let us take heed to the Holy Spirit's warning of Jezebel's plot:

PROVERBS 7:24–27 NKJV

Now therefore, listen to me, my children; pay attention to the words of my mouth:

Do not let your heart turn aside to her ways, do not stray into her paths;

For she has cast down many wounded, and all who were slain by her were strong men.

Her house is the way to hell, descending to the chambers of death.

LIFESAVING PRACTICES FOR PREVENTING MORAL FAILURE[28]

Recognize Your Vulnerability

Sexual temptation is no respecter of persons, of denominational labels, or of leadership positions. Ministers who recognize the powerful force against which they battle in ministry will live with the frightening but motivating knowledge that they *could* commit sexual immorality. Consequently, they should take precautions to prevent this from happening to them.

Guard Your Heart

Sexual sin is often the result of progressive steps. One of those progressive steps may be a failure to keep your first love—your love relationship with the Lord. Regular, honest check-ups of your relationship with Him can prevent this from happening.

---

[28] http://enrichmentjournal.ag.org/200504/200504_040_sb_lifesaving.cfm.

Guard Your Mind

Immorality is the cumulative product of small mental indulgences and seemingly minor compromises, the immediate consequences of which were, at the time, indiscernible. Our thoughts are the fabric with which we weave our character and destiny. When an impure thought thrusts itself into a person's consciousness, he can choose not to dwell on it but instead replace it with something good or just.

Guard Your Marriage

Being in love with one's spouse provides the best defense against sexual misconduct. We must intentionally engage in activities that will help build strong marriages and meet each other's top emotional needs.

Practical suggestions for guarding your marriage include surrounding your work environment with reminders of your spouse and children through their pictures, drawings, and other mementos, and learning to only speak highly of your spouse in public.

Guard Your Computer

In recent surveys by *Christianity Today* and *Leadership Journal,* 33 percent of clergy responded that they had visited a sexually explicit website within the last year, and 18 percent of these admitted to visiting sexually explicit sites between a couple of times a month to more than once a week.

Pornography is not "harmless fun" that doesn't hurt anyone. It's a dehumanized, synthetic version of sex that eliminates love, honor, dignity, intimacy, and commitment. The use of pornography is a self-centered, consuming experience that disconnects the person from God, from his spouse and family, and from his own feelings. The damaging effects of pornography on our lives, our families, and God's Kingdom are immeasurable.

Recognize and Address the Warning Signs

Know yourself, including your own risk factors and warning signs. The instant you recognize signals from a member of the opposite sex, call it for what it is and consciously put preventive measures in place. A relationship can be headed in the wrong direction long before it becomes sexual. One of the most important responses to these subtle warning signs is to back off early. Emotions are controllable. Ministers must keep a tight rein on their feelings at all times.

Hold Yourself Accountable to Others

Accountability among ministers is critically important, yet most fail to seek it out. Many pastors in small churches feel isolated, and even those in large churches with many staff members can be lone rangers when it comes to facing their moral struggles. It is imperative that ministers find others—whether staff members, laity, or other ministers—who will love them as they are and regularly ask questions that will keep them accountable.

Regularly Rehearse the Consequences

Ministers would do well to write out their own list of specific consequences that would result from sexual immorality. As they consider the consequences—the anxiety, shame, and regret—they might want to visualize themselves standing in front of their spouse or church and confessing what they have done. They should regularly review the causes and consequences of sexual misconduct. In a tangible and personal way, doing this brings home God's inviolate law of choice and consequence, cutting through the fog of rationalization and filling our hearts with the healthy, motivating fear of God.

Keep Purity a Priority

I read a very powerful booklet by Dr. Don Gossett on moral purity for ministers and the people of God. He shared some sad stories of ministers who fell into moral impurity and adultery. Some of these men were mightily used by God during the healing revival days of the 1960s.

He wrote, "Nothing will plunge a ministry from the mountain of usefulness like impurity."[29] He wrote further, "It is important to discern when Satan is trying to snare you by unclean spirits."

---

[29] Don Gossett, *Purity Is Power* (BAC Printers, Singapore. 1992), 4.

"I've witnessed these seducing spirits work against good people who never considered committing adultery. These evil powers subtly manifest themselves to break down resistance, to make impurity appear alluring and desirable. To overcome these attacks, an all-out warfare must be waged by boldly quoting God's Word against him. The devil has scattered immoral people all over; he wants to choose your body and mind as one he drops unsound thoughts and seductive persons who endeavor to cause you to be added to his casualty list. Keep the anointing of the Holy Spirit flowing at flood tide so you can overcome the avalanche of unclean spirits arrayed against Christians."

Never Again Confession[30]

1. Never again will I confess that I can't stay pure; instead, "I can do all things through Christ who strengthens me" (Philippians 4:13 NKJV).
2. Never again will I confess a fear of Satan's traps overtaking me, for "God has not given us a spirit of fear, but of power and of love and of a sound mind" (2 Timothy 1:7 NKJV).
3. Never again will I confess moral weakness in moral matters, for "the LORD is the strength of my life" (Psalm 27:1 NKJV).
4. Never will I confess the supremacy of the filthy, unclean spirits unleashed in this world against my life, for I declare with Jesus: "the prince of this world cometh, and hath nothing in me" (John 14:30 KJV).

[30] Ibid., 51.

5. Never again will I confess defeat in maintaining purity, for "God…always causeth us to triumph in Christ" (2 Corinthians 2:14 KJV).
6. Never again will I confess bondage to unclean spirits, for "where the Spirit of the Lord is, there is liberty" (2 Corinthians 3:17 KJV). My body is the pure dwelling place of the Holy Spirit.

LANDMINE # 5 THE CANCER OF PRIDE

MARK 7:21–23 AMPC

For from within, [that is] out of the hearts of men, come base and wicked thoughts, sexual immorality, stealing, murder, adultery, coveting (a greedy desire to have more wealth), dangerous and destructive wickedness, deceit; unrestrained (indecent) conduct; an evil eye (envy), slander (evil speaking, malicious misrepresentation, abusiveness), pride (the sin of an uplifted heart against God and man), foolishness (folly, lack of sense, recklessness, thoughtlessness).

All these evil [purposes and desires] come from within, and they make the man unclean and render him unhallowed.

"Pride is the only disease known to man that makes everyone sick except the one who has it."

—Author Unknown

Pride is like cancer—before you can see it visibly, it grows inside in secret. You can see its symptoms a little, but you cannot exactly predict how much of the disease has taken root inside. The dictionary defines *pride* as "a high or inordinate opinion of one's own dignity, importance, merit, or superiority, whether as cherished in the mind or displayed in bearing, conduct, etc."[31]

God hates pride (Proverbs 8:13). He stands personally against it (Proverbs 16:5). He does not tolerate it (1 Peter 5:5). He considers the person of pride to be an abomination (Proverbs 16:5). The Lord will destroy the house of the proud (Proverbs 15:25). The hand of God will be absent in the house of the prideful. The family members will become vulnerable to the attacks of the enemy. I have seen so many of such families; if either father or mother has a prideful heart and a sharp tongue that brings strife in the church, their children carry the same disease of pride. Why? The children are brought up in the house of the proud. The absence of humility and of the fragrance of the presence of God makes room for the foul odor of demons.

Pride leads to destruction (Proverbs 16:8). Pride is like a double-edged sword of the devil working within the heart of man; it kills others by bringing about contention (Proverbs 13:10), and it kills you by bringing humiliation and disgrace (Proverbs 11:2; 29:23).

Pride has the ability to keep you unteachable by bringing a false sense of security—a false dependence on self (Obadiah 3:3). Pride has the ability to take you far away from God (Psalm 138:6

[31] *Webster's New Universal Unabridged Dictionary.*

NLT). Pride self-educates you apart from the Holy Spirit. That's why we have problems with many church folks who use the Bible to bring disunity within the congregation, just like the folks did in the church at Corinth (Proverbs 28:25; 1 Corinthians 10–12).

Pride will cause you to fight against the anointing. You will start fighting against anyone who carries an anointing of God that you don't have yourself (Psalm 86:14; 119:51, 69, 85). Pride is the very breeding ground for Jezebel's activity. The spirit of Jezebel has to insinuate pride so that the very pride itself fights against the Elijahs, the anointed ones!

Pride was the womb from which Satan was born. God created Lucifer as an angel of the Lord, but he became Satan by himself, on his own. How was that possible? The Bible gives us some indication in Isaiah 14:12–15 of how Lucifer went through the birth canal of pride by trying to exalt himself against the Almighty God. This is the reason that pride hates the true anointing; it is like saying Satan hates God!

Joyce Meyer said it well: "While the world is busy trying to conquer the outer space, we should strive to conquer the inner space of the heart within,"[32] and "God is more concerned about our heart than He is of our performance because if our heart is right, our performance will eventually catch up with that. But if we go around doing the right things with a wrong heart, what we do doesn't mean anything to God."[33]

---

[32] Joyce Meyer, *The Making of a Leader* (Tulsa: Harrison House, 2001), 70.
[33] Ibid., 70.

HUMILITY

I went to a Christian bookshop in Australia wanting to buy some books. As I walked toward the main entrance, there were many books on a table with low-priced clearance tags. One book caught my attention: The title of the book was *Humility* by C. Peter Wagner. I grabbed the book straightaway, not for the price but because of the title. Any book on humility is a prized possession in my library.

Is it little wonder that people don't like the concept of humility? What a shame it is when the people of God shun the very fragrance of heaven, the spirit of humility. This book by Dr. Wagner contains an excellent chapter entitled "Five Signposts Along the Road to Pride."[34] I will quote from two of these signposts of pride for our study here:

- Signpost 1—Yearning for Praise and Human Accolades: "Being the object of praise does not necessarily cause pride. But yearning for praise can very rapidly lead to pride. One way to avoid this is to acknowledge praise but not to enjoy too much of it."[35]
- Signpost 4—Rejoicing in Others' Failures and Resenting Others' Successes: "The soil that nourishes this root of pride is carnal competition."[36]

---

[34] C. Peter Wagner, *Humility* (Ventura, Calif.: Regal Books, 2002), 59.
[35] Ibid., 63.
[36] Ibid., 70.

Dr. Wagner writes much about competition between ministers and churches, which is an absolute violation of the spirit of unity and love. He further quotes Andrew Murray: "The humble man feels no jealousy or envy. He can praise God when others are preferred and blessed before him. He can bear to hear others praised and himself forgotten, because in God's presence he has learned to say with Paul, 'I am nothing' (2 Corinthians 12:11)."[37] "Part of humility is a willingness to be underestimated or slighted and to feel no resentment."[38]

In this present time of the revival of the "Apostolic Revolution," many are fighting over their spiritual identities. Many ministers feel that if they don't identify themselves as one in the movement, no one will accept or respect them.

"While the use of titles can be important, even essential, in some cultures, such as those parts of Asia, in our American culture, the lust for titles can be a symptom of pride. Some people hold titles as a prized possession, and they are a bit offended when the desired term, perhaps 'doctor,' 'bishop,' 'pastor,' or 'apostle,' is not used.

"This is often the case among individuals who are insecure and who attempt, through insisting on titles, to build a self-assuring case of superiority."[39] The sentry of your heart's door is called "humility." Dismiss that guardian, and your unprotected gate will soon be battered in, with the enemy taking over.[40]

---

37 Andrew Murray, *Humility* (New Kensington, PA: Whitaker House, 1982), 20.

38 C. Peter Wagner. *Humility* (Ventura, Calif.: Regal Books, 2002), 71.

39 Ibid., 65–66.

40 Reinhard Bonnke, *Evangelism by Fire* (Full Flame GmbH, 2001), 269.

KINGDOM CULTURE

The problem with pride is that it is found everywhere, across all cultures. We are called by God to walk in humility, not in comparison to our family of origin, but rather out of our Kingdom culture.

LUKE 9:46–48 AMPC

But a controversy arose among them as to which of them might be the greatest [surpassing the others in excellence, worth, and authority]. But Jesus, as He perceived the thoughts of their hearts, took a little child and put him at His side and told them, Whoever receives and accepts and welcomes this child in My name and for My sake receives and accepts and welcomes Me; and whoever so receives Me so also receives Him Who sent Me. For he who is least and lowliest among you all—he is [the one who is truly] great.

My precious brothers and sisters in the Lord, do not become carriers of the spirit of pride. If you are a carrier, repent before the Lord. Offended people are often targeted by demons to become potential carriers of the spirit of pride, as the enemy uses them to destroy both themselves and the Church. The end-time army must walk in love and humility.

LANDMINE # 6
THE SPIRIT OF JEALOUSY

F. B. Meyer relayed the following experience to a few of his personal friends. "It was easy," he said, "to pray for the success of

G. Campbell Morgan when he was in America. But when he came back to England and took a church near to mine, it was something different. The old Adam in me was inclined to jealousy, but I got my heel upon his head, and whether I felt right toward my friend, I determined to act right.

"My church gave a reception for him, and I acknowledged that if it was not necessary for me to preach on Sunday evenings I would dearly love to go and hear him myself. Well, that made me feel right toward him. But just see how the dear Lord helped me out of my difficulty. There was Charles Spurgeon preaching wonderfully on the other side of me. He and Mr. Morgan were so popular, and drew such crowds, that our church caught the overflow, and we had all we could accommodate" (Ministers' Research Service).

Another trap the enemy sets against the believers and ministers is the spirit of jealousy. The spirit of pride propels this demonic spirit of jealousy. While praying in my room, I was permitted by the Lord to see the form of this demon. This spirit takes the form of a woman. Its eyes were full of evil and pride. Its eyes were controlling the entire movement of its body, just like a snake that moves and slithers to the places it sees. This demon was even wearing a covering over its head, like a shawl; to portray the picture of innocence, yet it is vile within. I saw this demon standing near the doorway, looking straight at me. There was so much evil within her very being. The eyes of this spirit were like the eyes of a serpent. I was able to discern cunningness, betrayal, and adultery coming out from her.

2 CORINTHIANS 11:3 AMPC

But [now] I am fearful, lest that even as the serpent beguiled Eve by his cunning, so your minds may be corrupted and seduced from wholehearted and sincere and pure devotion to Christ.

This demon spirit is jealous of believers who are walking right and strong in holiness before the Lord. She will attempt to tempt the child of God to sin against the holiness of God and stain their garments of righteousness.

When the Church walks in unity, this demon spirit of jealousy takes its assignment from Satan to cause dissension and strife among the church members. It uses those who walk in carnality within the Church as bait to stir up problems (1 Corinthians 3:3; 2 Timothy 2:23). Even carnal ministers can become a tool in the hands of this spirit. These ministers will block the work of the Holy Spirit in their churches.

THE EYE OF JEALOUSY

1 SAMUEL 18:6–9

When the men were returning home after David had killed the Philistine, the women came out from all the towns of Israel to meet King Saul with singing and dancing, with joyful songs and with tambourines and lutes.

As they danced, they sang: "Saul has slain his thousands, and David his tens of thousands."

Saul was very angry; this refrain galled him. "They have credited David with tens of thousands," he thought, "but me with only thousands. What more can he get but the kingdom?"

And from that time on Saul kept a jealous eye on David.

Anger and resentment within the heart of Saul qualified him as a prime candidate to host the spirit of jealousy. Saul harbored so much fear (1 Samuel 18:12, 29) against David that fear drove him to hunt for David. Saul was so demonically energized that thoughts of anger and murder overpowered him. When Saul came to know that his daughter Michal was in love with David, he was pleased. He planned to give his daughter to David so that she might become a snare to him (1 Samuel 18:21). What a father!

That's what the spirit of jealousy does! It robs people of the fear of God, along with honor and respect for servants of God. Those carrying this spirit will do anything to cause confusion in the church if they are not in control or in leadership. When their voices are not heard, the spirit of jealousy will start a "whisper campaign" in the church (Jeremiah 9:8). The spirit of jealousy has only one assignment—to bring about confusion and disorder and to break apart relationships (James 3:16).

PROVERBS 16:28 NKJV

A perverse man sows strife, and a whisperer separates the best of friends.

Many divine relationships and God-ordained connections have been aborted through the operation of the spirit of jealousy.

The spirit of fear will cause jealousy to spring up when someone who can serve just like them comes to church. Think about it. First, the spirit of fear robs you the opportunity to serve God; next, the same spirit will bring anger and jealousy when others come forward to serve. There are many people like Saul in the church. The spirit of fear and jealousy will cause self-inflicted emotions of rejection in wounded hearts. These hearts are the nesting ground for these spirits to incubate. The spirit of fear will impose fear on others and infects them to steal their freedom.

Praise be to God! No matter how hard the enemy tries to trap believers, God uses those very circumstances to lift His children up. Saul was plotting an evil plan against David, which involved asking for a hundred foreskins of the Philistines. This would greatly increase the chances of David dying in battle. But God protected him and gave him success, and David's name soon became well known (1 Samuel 18:28–30).

DETONATING THE LANDMINES

You cannot stop the enemy from setting landmines against the soldiers of Christ—but through the wisdom of God, we can identify and avoid those traps. Our mission is to keep the Church and her people, the soldiers of Christ, alive.

EPHESIANS 4:16 NLT

He makes the whole body fit together perfectly. As each part does its own special work, it helps the other parts grow, so that the whole body is healthy and growing and full of love.

Satan is afraid of a church that actively engages its people to do the works of God (1 Corinthians 12:24–27). When the people do their part according to the plan of God, the Church becomes a strong and healthy fighting force through the working of the Holy Spirit in and through it. The power of God's love holds the Church and her people together in the spirit of unity and the bond of peace (Ephesians 4:3).

As the army of God, we must stay alert in our hearts to the inner workings of the Holy Spirit and become fervent in our walk with Him (Romans 12:11; 2 Timothy 1:6). It is time that we show our talk through our actions (James 2:17). Our faith and our actions must work together if we are to ever experience overcoming faith and victory.

Reinhard Bonnke wrote, "You know, 'Armchair Christians' receive no fire. There is no such thing as an 'anointed couch potato.' Sometimes people pray for fire when they are not yielded to God at all, and subsequently, they do little for Him.

"One day a lady told me there was a 'demon' sitting on her. At the same time, she said she was a born-again Christian. I said to her, 'Flies can only sit on a cold stove, so get the fire of God in your life and any demon that touches you will burn his filthy fingers.'

The Gospel provides its own fiery power. Make sure it's ignited in your soul."[41]

WHAT MUST I DO TO OVERCOME TRAPS?

> **"We need pure hearts, pure motives, and God's anointing upon our eyes to perceive the snares of the devil."**[42]
>
> —Reinhard Bonnke

JOHN 16:33 AMPC

I have told you these things, so that in Me you may have [perfect] peace and confidence. In the world you have tribulation and trials and distress and frustration; but be of good cheer [take courage; be confident, certain, undaunted]! For I have overcome the world. [I have deprived it of power to harm you and have conquered it for you.]

As our Lord Jesus has said, we, as His soldiers, are to take courage and be confident in His keeping power (Psalm 18:28; 1 Peter 1:5). He has deprived the world of its evil power to overcome us. However, there are some necessary steps we can take to walk in the spirit of liberty.

---

41 Reinhard Bonnke, *Monthly Partners Letter* (Full Flame, September/SGP, 2005), 1–2.

42 Reinhard Bonnke, *Evangelism by Fire* (Full Flame GmbH, 2001), 245.

BE IN GOD'S PROTECTION

PSALM 31:4 NKJV

Pull me out of the net which they have secretly laid for me, for You are my strength.

Walk in the protection of God. If you would so desire to walk right before Him in holiness and in truth, the Lord will commission His angels to look after you (Psalm 34:7; 91:11; Proverbs 14:26). Even when Satan tries to lure you when you are not alert, the Lord's watchfulness will guard you (Psalm 121:3–4).

The name of the Lord is the strong tower in which you must abide. There is safety in His name (Proverbs 18:10). Dwell in the Scriptures. Stay under the shadow of the Almighty (Psalm 91:1). Satan will try his best to advance against the soldiers of the Lord. His sole aim is to lure us outside of the protection of God. Satan could not harm Job because of the hedge of God's protection over his life (Job 1:10).

Don't let the devil tempt you ever to serve God in another "good idea" ministry. Stay close to the right people whom the Lord has connected you with. Many ministers' eyes of the spirit are so weak that they cannot see those whom the Lord has sent across their path. They work along with those they shouldn't, and they refuse to work with those whom they should, from heaven's point of view.

In addition, don't be tempted by the devil to fight a war that is not yours. The Lord knows your spiritual strength. All the troubles in the natural and the battles in the Spirit are permitted for your growth, according to your inner strength of the heart and the spirit (Psalm 25:17a). He will not allow any trouble to kill you (1 Corinthians 10:13), although that's what the enemy attempts to do. The battle is always the Lord's—not yours (2 Chronicles 20:15). The devil will tempt you to think that you are the answer to every battle, not the Lord. If you are harboring such thoughts, it is a symptom of hidden pride that is growing within you. Cut it off. Come back under the protection of God. Many people in the Bible forfeited the protection of God by continuously living a lifestyle of disobedience.

Disobedience is the most effective tool the enemy of our souls has to use against the Body of Christ at large (1 Samuel 15:22–23). Think of Saul. His seeming obedience was "right in his own eyes." But in the eyes of the Lord, it was absolute disobedience to a direct command of the Lord given through His prophet (1 Samuel 15:10). Disobedience snatches you out of the hedge of God's protection.

Sir Leonard Wood once visited the king of France. The king was so pleased with him that he was invited for dinner with the king the next day. Sir Leonard went to the palace, and the king, meeting him in one of the halls, said, "Why, Sir Leonard, I did not expect to see you. How is it that you are here?" "Did not Your Majesty invite me to dine with you?" said the astonished guest. "Yes," replied the king, "but you did not answer my invitation." It was then that Sir Leonard Wood uttered one of the choicest sentences of his life. He replied, "A king's invitation is never to be answered, but to be obeyed."

I want to encourage you—make every effort to walk in obedience to the will of God. Don't struggle against God. Obey Him. He loves you.

DON'T LIVE IN SIN

ECCLESIASTES 7:26

I find more bitter than death the woman who is a snare, whose heart is a trap and whose hands are chains. The man who pleases God will escape her, but the sinner she will ensnare.

The enemy, like a seductress, comes with snares and traps. The Bible says that even the heart of the seductress is a trap. Perhaps it is speaking of the false love and hope that the seductress will use as assurance to those who are about to fall into her web. Her hands carry the chain that seeks to imprison your service for God. Your hands will be useless once they are chained.

This is the picture of the seductress in Proverbs 7:21: "With persuasive words she led him astray; she seduced him with her smooth talk." The Amplified Bible, Classic Edition, says she will seduce him "[to overcome his conscience and his fears] and forces him along."

I cannot help but think of Samson lying down upon the lap of Delilah: She said to him, "How can you say, 'I love you,' when you won't confide in me? This is the third time you have made a fool of me and haven't told me the secret of your great strength." With such nagging she prodded him day after day until he was tired to death. So he told her everything" (Judges 16:15–17).

The saddest verse in the life of Samson speaks of when the Holy Spirit left him—and he did not even know it (Judges 16:20). Oh! How much more we must live a life of holiness and walk in the fear of God! No wonder David cried out before Almighty God, "Create in me a clean heart, O God, and renew a steadfast spirit within me. Do not cast me away from Your presence, and do not take Your Holy Spirit from me" (Psalm 51:10–11 NKJV).

1 CORINTHIANS 9:27 AMPC

But [like a boxer] I buffet my body [handle it roughly, discipline it by hardships] and subdue it, for fear that after proclaiming to others the Gospel and things pertaining to it, I myself should become unfit [not stand the test, be unapproved and rejected as a counterfeit].

How many people in the Church have been disqualified by being overwhelmed by a lifestyle of sin? Many, like Judas, judge themselves as being unworthy of serving God (Matthew 27:3–5). But the very act of self-judgment, though it gives a "sincere" picture of your grief toward sin, is a sin nevertheless. None of us are commanded to pass self-judgment and self-abort the call of God.

Come to the cleansing blood of Jesus. Confess your sins and shortcomings. He will forgive you, cleanse you, and restore His grace toward your life (Psalm 51:7; 1 Peter 5:10; 1 John 1:9).

LIVE A LIFESTYLE OF TESTIMONY

1 TIMOTHY 3:7 NKJV

Moreover he must have a good testimony among those who are outside, lest he fall into reproach and the snare of the devil.

I am writing now to those who desire to be all that God wants them to be. I am addressing those of you who are madly in love with Jesus and the will of the Father—so much so that you are willing to do anything for this divine, heavenly love.

If you want to be a soldier in the army of Jesus, then get used to training hard for the Lord. Keep your spirit strong, your soul renewed, and your lifestyle transformed by the power of God. Don't go around whining and complaining that "God is too hard on me" or that "it is so difficult to pray. I don't understand the Bible."

Jesus said, "If anyone desires to be My disciple, let him deny himself [disregard, lose sight of, and forget himself and his own interests] and take up his cross and follow Me [cleave steadfastly to Me, conform wholly to My example in living and, if need be, in dying, also] (Matthew 16:24 AMPC).

Stop pampering your flesh, and for a change, listen to what God has to say about your life. When you consistently walk the lifestyle of a disciple, you can overcome the snares of the enemy. Many are getting tired of living a godly and "restricted" lifestyle in the flesh. Some believers feel their leaders are too legalistic about the Christian disciplines.

The echoes of many "churchgoers" are, "Why can't I go to the pub?" "What's wrong with flirting?" My friends, you cannot afford to sleep with the enemy and dance in the church. The devil will use you as the very tool to cause many others to stumble.

Paul gave the Corinthian church a hard pill to swallow. The people of Corinth were living a permissive lifestyle. There were new converts who had to be taught the Bible's view on their social life, including rules for marriage (1 Corinthians 7), the idea of liberty (1 Corinthians 8, 10), instruction on personal priorities (1 Corinthians 9), and many others. For instance, many of them ate food that had been offered to idols. As the mature Christians were enjoying their liberty without the balance of responsibility, many young converts were stumbling in their walk with Christ. Paul had to address this issue.

1 CORINTHIANS 8:12–13 AMPC

And when you sin against your brethren in this way, wounding and damaging their weak conscience, you sin against Christ.

Therefore, if [my eating a] food is a cause of my brother's falling or of hindering [his spiritual advancement], I will not eat [such] flesh forever, lest I cause my brother to be tripped up and fall and to be offended.

As a disciple, a lover of God, you must choose to be careful and sensitive about how you conduct your life in this world. The Bible instructs us to live a life worthy of the Gospel (Philippians 1:27), to be an example in speech, in conduct, in love, in spirit, in faith, and in purity (1 Timothy 4:12), and to be without covetousness by being content with what God has blessed us with (Hebrews 13:5).

LUKE 21:34

Be careful, or your hearts will be weighed down with dissipation, drunkenness and the anxieties of life, and that day will close on you unexpectedly like a trap.

My fellow brothers and sisters, as soldiers, you must get used to the word "sacrifice." As someone has said, "Sacrifice is the ecstasy of giving the best we have to the one we love the most."

Oswald Sanders wrote, "If we are willing to give up only wrong things for Jesus, never let us talk of being in love with Him. Anyone will give up wrong things if he knows how, but are we prepared to give up the best we have for Jesus Christ? The only right a Christian has is the right to give up his rights. If we are to be the best for God, there must be victory in the realm of legitimate desire as well as in the realm of unlawful indulgence."[43]

[43] J. Oswald Sanders, *Spiritual Discipleship* (Chicago: Moody Bible Institute, 1990), 106.

LIVE IN THE WORD AND IN THE FEAR OF THE LORD

PROVERBS 14:27 NKJV

The fear of the LORD is a fountain of life, to turn one away from the snares of death.

PROVERBS 19:23

The fear of the LORD leads to life: then one rests content, untouched by trouble.

The Word of God will become the truth that protects you from the snares of the enemy. The religious leaders of Jesus' day were unable to trap Him when He taught at the temple. And every time they tried to trap Him, Jesus answered with the wisdom of the Father, and they became silent (Luke 20:26).

2 CORINTHIANS 5:10

For we must all appear before the judgment seat of Christ, that each one may receive what is due him for the things done while in the body, whether good or bad.

Knowing we must all appear before the judgment seat of Christ and give an account of the deeds done while we were in the body, let us walk in the fear of the Lord.

May our Lord Jesus give you wisdom and strength to stand against all the wiles of the enemy and overcome all the landmines that come against your life. Walk in courage always knowing that:

ISAIAH 54:17 AMPC

But no weapon that is formed against you shall prosper, and every tongue that shall rise against you in judgment you shall show to be in the wrong. This [peace, righteousness, security, triumph over opposition] is the heritage of the servants of the Lord [those in whom the ideal Servant of the Lord is reproduced]; this is the righteousness or the vindication which they obtain from Me [this is that which I impart to them as their justification], says the Lord.

OPS BRIEFING 4

WEARY SAINTS AND TIRED SOLDIERS

Once upon a time, it was announced that the devil was going out of business and would sell all his equipment to those who were willing to pay the price. On the day of the big sale, all his tools were attractively displayed.

The tools included: Envy, Jealousy, Hatred, Malice, Deceit, Sensuality, Pride, Idolatry, and other implements of evil display. Each of the tools were marked with their own price tag. Over in the corner by itself was a harmless-looking, wedge-shaped tool, very much worn out, but still it bore a higher price than any of the others.

Someone asked the devil what it was, and he answered, "That is Discouragement." The next question came quickly, "And why is it priced so high, even though it is plain to see that it is worn out more than these others?" "Because," replied the devil, "it is more useful to me than all of these others.

"I can pry open and get into a man's heart with that when I cannot get near him with any other tool. Once I get inside, I can use him in whatever way suits me best. It is worn out because I use it on everyone, and few people even know it belongs to me." This tool was priced so high that no one could buy it, and to this day, it has never been sold. It still belongs to the devil, and he still uses it on mankind.

All of us can relate to discouragement. Those who serve in the ministry are more prone to get discouraged than the average person, it seems. It would be a lie to say that we will not get discouraged at all if we pray more, fast more, or be more obedient to God. Rather, it is wise and right to identify the source of our discouragement and learn appropriate ways to manage valid discouragement and discard illegal discouragement.

DISCOURAGEMENT LOCKS YOUR ANOINTING

1 KINGS 19:1–5 NKJV

And Ahab told Jezebel all that Elijah had done, also how he had executed all the prophets with the sword.

Then Jezebel sent a messenger to Elijah, saying, "So let the gods do to me, and more also, if I do not make your life as the life of one of them by tomorrow about this time."

And when he saw that, he arose and ran for his life, and went to Beersheba, which belongs to Judah, and left his servant there.

But he himself went a day's journey into the wilderness, and came and sat down under a broom tree. And he prayed that he might die, and said, "It is enough! Now, Lord, take my life, for I am no better than my fathers!"

Then as he lay and slept under a broom tree, suddenly an angel touched him, and said to him, "Arise and eat."

Have you ever said those "magic" words, "I have had enough!"? We all have at some point, and some of us have done exceptionally well in speaking those words regularly in response to every single thing. Yes, these were the very words that came from the mouth of Elijah, the mighty prophet of God.

If you have ever spoken these words, repent now before the Lord. By your own words, you have locked up your anointing and have become a prisoner to your soul (Proverbs 18:21). Your words have become a snare to your life (Proverbs 18:7).

Once discouragement sets in, you will lose focus on the goal God has set for your life. The momentum of your walk in Christ will slow down, possibly to the point of your backsliding, unless you press forward (Philippians 3:12–14). You will now choose to sit behind and relax in the church instead of serving the Lord. You will tend to come to church and then leave immediately rather than wait to fellowship with others in the church.

Some will say, "It's their fault that I am like this." Allow me to warn you as the Lord's servant: regardless of who you are or in what capacity you have served the Lord, if you choose to walk away from the call of God, you will be judged on the choice you have made. Jesus warned, "No one, having put his hand to the plow, and looking back, is fit for the kingdom of God" (Luke 9:62 NKJV).

Elijah witnessed the greatest miracle ever in his life and ministry on Mount Carmel. He saw the fire of God falling on a wet altar (1 Kings 18:38). He saw how powerless the prophets of Baal were in his presence. The authority of the anointing of God was strong on him as he challenged and ridiculed the prophets and priests of Baal, whom he later slaughtered. Nobody could stand before Elijah. He was the man of the day.

Yet, after witnessing such a powerful display of God's might, just at one word of threat from Jezebel, Elijah ran for his life. Why? How was that possible? Where was God? What happened to all the courage Elijah had displayed earlier? At one stage, the power of the Lord came upon Elijah, and he ran ahead of Ahab's chariot. Now he was running for his life. What a contrast of personality!

Did Elijah get tired and weary after all the spiritual warfare he had fought throughout the day? Maybe he had hoped that when Ahab gave Jezebel news of the massacre of her false prophets, she would repent. And Israel would then have a chance to worship the living God without the idolatrous practices of Jezebel.

On the contrary, Jezebel sent a message to Elijah. As Dr. Warren W. Wiersbe writes: "Jezebel wasn't only an evil woman; she was also a shrewd strategist who knew how to make the most of Baal's defeat on Mount Carmel."[44]

---

[44] Warren Wiersbe, *The Bible Exposition Commentary* (Colorado Springs: Victor, 2003), 476.

Interestingly, the King James Version of 1 Kings 19:3 states, "And **when he saw** that, he arose, and went for his life, and came to Beersheba, which belongeth to Judah, and left his servant there" (emphasis mine). The Septuagint reads, "he was afraid." The newer translations have adopted the latter phrase. The question remains, what was it that Elijah saw that made him afraid?

During a battle in ancient days, it was customary for war generals to cut off the head of the general who lost to display their victory. On seeing the head lifted and on hearing the sound of the trumpet, the soldiers would stop fighting. The defeated army would then surrender, and in most cases, be killed. That was the case when Goliath was beheaded by David in 1 Samuel 17:50–54. The Bible states that David brought the head of Goliath to Jerusalem.

This tactic generated much fear in the hearts of the opposing forces, and this act of terror remained in practice in many regiments of the ancient world. During the Iraq War, terrorists took many hostages and beheaded some of them. The terrorists recorded the cruelty on video and televised it around the world. After imposing such fear, they then would make their demands.

Elijah had all the false prophets slaughtered. Upon hearing the news, King Ahab could have ordered his soldiers to look through the slaughter place. As evidence, the soldiers could have brought back the head of the chief priest. Upon seeing the head, Jezebel could have burst out in anger. She could then have sent the head of the slaughtered priest together with a message to Elijah. And the message is found in the text: "So let the gods do to me, and more also, if I do not make your life as the life of one of them by tomorrow about this time." The Bible states that Elijah "**saw** and he **was afraid**."

Commenting on this passage, Dr. Wiersbe wrote, "The combination of emotional burnout, weariness, hunger, and a deep sense of failure, plus lack of faith in the Lord, had brought Elijah into deep depression."[45]

Brethren, we must keep in mind that any one of us could have done the same thing or even worse if we were put in the same spot as Elijah. The Bible says that Elijah was a man just like us (James 5:17).

ELIJAH! YOU ARE NOT A FAILURE!

Elijah's reaction was an example of what every minister has done during moments of discouragement, fear, and depression. Elijah ran to meet God. It was as though the Lord was expecting him to run to Him. Maybe the Lord had already seen Elijah's weariness and drew him to the presence of God to strengthen him for the next phase of his life and ministry.

No work truly done for God will ever be wasted (Isaiah 55:11). God remembers your sacrifices, your tears, your prayers, and the times you spent waiting on Him. It's all on record!

God called my elder brother, Sadhu Sundar Selvaraj, in a supernatural way to preach the Gospel to the Tibetans.[46] He has been

---

[45] Warren Wiersbe, *The Bible Exposition Commentary* (Colorado Springs: Victor, 2003), 477.

[46] For more information, visit http://www.jesusministries.org.

evangelizing among the Tibetans for the past twenty years. Tibet, being a nation whose doors are closed to the outside world, has outlawed every form of evangelism. My brother often tells me of how he was supernaturally protected by angels when the officials caught him for preaching to the monks.

During a prayer meeting, my brother shared this account, which moved me to tears. Someone asked him, "You are saying that you have been preaching the Gospel for these many years, but where are the converts?" On hearing this, my brother was not able to give an answer, as many of the Tibetans who had accepted Christ were living as secret Christians.

He then told of how he brought the matter before God, sobbing with tears. He said, "Lord, these many years I have gone to Tibet to preach Your Word faithfully. I have suffered much physically during the course of this work, but Lord, I have not seen the result with my eyes." As he cried his heart out before the feet of Jesus, the Lord appeared to him in a supernatural way.

The Lord said, "Son, when you come into My Kingdom, you will see countless numbers of Tibetans there as a result of your work. None of the work you have done will be wasted." On hearing that account that day in the church, I sobbed in the presence of the Lord, thinking of His love and mercy toward His servants.

PSALM 126:5–6 AMPC

They who sow in tears shall reap in joy and singing. He who goes forth bearing seed and weeping [at needing his precious supply of grain for sowing] shall doubtless come again with rejoicing, bringing his sheaves with him.

Certainly, Elijah was not a failure. If God could have considered his running away as a grave sin, He would not have sent an angel to warn him. Rather, an angel of the Lord came to lift him up and sustain him with food. The Lord sent a high-ranking angel to encourage His beloved servant, who had become exhausted and tired. Elijah was ready to die and give up his ministry, but the Lord renewed and restored him.

1 KINGS 19:7–9 NKJV

And the angel of the LORD came back the second time, and touched him, and said, "Arise and eat, because the journey is too great for you." So he arose, and ate and drank; and he went in the strength of that food forty days and forty nights as far as Horeb, the mountain of God. And there he went into a cave, and spent the night in that place; and behold, the word of the LORD came to him, and He said to him, "What are you doing here, Elijah?"

When Elijah fled to Mount Horeb, he was returning to the sacred place where God had met Moses and had given His laws to the people. The journey to Mount Horeb was about 200 miles (about 322 kilometers). In other words, the Lord sent him off in divine fasting for forty days and nights, just like He had sent Moses to do. Millennia later, Jesus met Moses and Elijah together on a mountaintop, as recorded in Luke 9:28–36.

YOUR MINISTRY CONTINUES

Elijah was commissioned to anoint three others as part of his new commissioning—Hazael, king over Aram; Jehu, king over Israel; and Elisha, to succeed Elijah as prophet (1 Kings 19:15–16). These men were to finish what the Lord had started through Elijah.

The Lord requires us, His servants, to complete the individual race set for each one of us (Acts 20:24; 1 Corinthians 9:24; 2 Timothy 4:7; Hebrews 12:1), but we cannot complete the Lord's race. The Lord Jesus' work will be completed when He reigns on the earth. Until then, the work goes on through each generation.

Each of us is continuing the ministry of someone else from a previous generation. This could be a surprise to some, but when you trace the history of the Bible, you will discover how the anointing and the commissioning gets passed down from one generation to the next to fulfill the will of the Father. Some servants of God know by revelation the mantle they have received from the Lord, while others have no knowledge of such. The important point is that each one of us must remain faithful to the call of God.

I remember praying for a minister friend concerning his ministry. As I prayed for him with much burden, the Lord showed me a vision. In this vision, I saw the mantle (anointing) of another minister, who had fallen due to some sin, come upon my friend. I cautiously shared with him what I saw in the Spirit. He shared with me how he had a dream like that which I had seen. And the Lord spoke to him that he was to continue the ministry of the fallen minister.

My brother, Sadhu Sundar Selvaraj, received the mantle of Sadhu Sundar Singh. He was told to continue Sundar Singh's ministry in Tibet. Sundar Singh had disappeared somewhere in the Himalayan mountains. Indian government agencies and Sundar Singh's close friends went on a search-and-rescue mission, but there was no trace of him found at all.

This is Sadhu Sundar Selvaraj's testimony:

> "On December 24, 1983, Brother Sadhu, as he is popularly and lovingly called, had a supernatural visitation from the Lord Jesus Christ. The Lord Jesus Christ appeared to him in the Spirit and began speaking to him about the legendary Sadhu Sundar Singh and Sadhu's ministry in Tibet. The Lord Jesus spoke to him for about twenty minutes. The Lord Jesus then asked Selvaraj, 'Will you continue that ministry?' Without any hesitation, Selvaraj answered 'Yes, Lord!' Smiling, the Lord said, 'Do not reply hastily! This is a very difficult ministry, with lots of suffering. You may have to suffer loneliness, isolation, hunger, pain, and persecution. Now tell Me. Will you accept this ministry?' Humbly kneeling before the Lord Jesus, Selvaraj answered, 'Yes, Lord. I will continue Sadhu Sundar Singh's ministry.' Pleased with that answer, the Lord Jesus came toward Selvaraj and placed a mantle on him. Laying His hands upon him, the Lord Jesus then said, 'I am ordaining you as an apostle to Tibet. Go and

evangelize Tibet and her people. From today you shall be called Sadhu Sundar Selvaraj.'"[47]

The Lord sends many servants to the nations of the world to pioneer mission works. When these servants have finished their work and have passed on to eternity, the anointing is then passed on to someone else to continue the mission. That said, the new minister and the ministry is not a copy of the former but rather a continuation of the former's mission as well as the commissioning the Lord gives to the present minister in each location.

Such was the case with my brother. Though he had received the mantle of Sadhu Sundar Singh, my brother was to continue what the former had started. There will be newer additions to that call. The Lord commissioned and mandated Sadhu in a supernatural encounter to begin a twenty-four-hour TV[48] station to preach the Second Coming of Jesus. Some observers who knew him well began to criticize his ministry, saying that he had gone off track and that he was no longer continuing Sadhu Sundar Singh's ministry. Keep in mind God wants us to *continue*, not *duplicate*.

Your ministry continues by the will of the Father, and no devil in hell can stop that. Lift up your head with the anointing of God and run in the name of Jesus. Do what the Lord has told you to do. Your ministry will continue. And when your time is over, the Lord will raise up someone else to finish what you have started. The work goes on until Jesus comes!

---

[47] http://www.jesusministries.org/tibetan.html.
[48] www.angeltv.org.

THE END-TIME MISSILE

My fellow comrades in the Lord's army, in these end times, the spirit of discouragement has been assigned to attack the servants of God and the believers to steal the call of God from their lives! Those who are accustomed to walk in the flesh, which allows their emotions to rule them, who do not put in much effort to walk in the love of God, will become the first victims.

The Lord revealed to me some years ago that one of the important assignments of demonic spirits is to steal "the salvation" of believers. You may be shocked to hear this. Perhaps you may be thinking, "Once I am saved, I don't have to bother with how I live. Jesus will always forgive me." Do not be deceived, brethren!

The Bible warns us to "work out (cultivate, carry out to the goal, and fully complete) your own salvation with reverence and awe and trembling (self-distrust, with serious caution, tenderness of conscience, watchfulness against temptation, timidly shrinking from whatever might offend God and discredit the name of Christ)" (Philippians 2:12 AMPC).

Unchallenged, this spirit takes prisoners. Satan has chosen this spirit of Jezebel to slow down and defeat the army of the Lord. To see you running is the sole desire of this demon. While many demonic spirits work from the outside, the spirit of discouragement camouflages itself within the human personality. If this is not dealt with at the right time, the pressure builds up, causing depression.

The spirit takes the "mood swings" in our human personality and uses them to its advantage. It will destroy its victims' walk with the Lord and then use those victims to cause discouragement in others. This was the case with Peter when he tried to dissuade Jesus from bearing the cross. But Jesus rebuked Satan, who was speaking through Peter (Matthew 16:23).

SHOCKING STATISTICS

Many ministers have lost their call and anointing due to discouragement. Many believers have left churches and are no longer active in their walk with God.

According to a survey conducted by the Fuller Institute of Church Growth in Pasadena, California,[49] these are some of the problems faced by pastors:

- 80 percent believe their ministry negatively affects their family.
- 70 percent have a lower self-esteem now than when they had first started the ministry.
- 40 percent have a serious conflict with a church member at least once a month.
- 70 percent do not have someone whom they would consider as a friend to confide in.

For many years, my heart was heavy with the burden given by Jesus for pastors and ministers. I wanted to minister the love of Jesus and the prophetic counsels from the Lord to them. After waiting for about seven years, the Lord opened the doors for me

---

[49] Chip Ricks, "How to Keep the Pastor You Love," article taken from http://www.bgcworld. org/mag/1005bgc/45.pdf.

in Indonesia, Australia, and Malaysia to organize camp meetings for pastors. We called it the Apostolic Empowerment Institute. To date, more than ten thousand pastors, ministers, and leaders have attended these camp meetings.

While in prayer, I once asked the Lord, "Lord, what is the central message I must bring to Your servants?" The Lord replied, "I want to encourage them. Tell them how much I appreciate them for being faithful in My work." Since then, a strong anointing has rested on me each time I conduct these camp meetings. During the anointing services, I have witnessed thousands of God's ministers in tears, weeping before the Lord as His love ministers to their hearts, giving them hope, promise, and a greater strength for the work of the Lord.

Many pastors come to the meetings with broken hearts and discouragement. Many of them minister in very poor conditions in the Indonesian islands, where there is much persecution. They lack the necessities of life and often face hardships for the sake of the Gospel. Many of them have asked, "Why is God blessing only the American churches with prosperity, but He does not listen to our prayers and our cries?" My heart has often been broken as I hear their stories and see their living conditions. Yes, these men and women may have felt like giving up many times, yet they remained steadfast in their call and their service to their Master.

Singapore has a population of 5.54 million people. According to a census taken in the year 2015,[50] 18.3 percent of the popula-

[50] http://www.singstat.gov.sg/keystats/c2000/wallchart.html#Religion.

tion are Christians, of whom 10.4 percent are Evangelicals.[51] This small island has been prophesied as being the Antioch of Asia, both in its sending of missionaries and in its financial support of missionary enterprises. We are blessed to have more than 1,500 registered churches and many more unregistered house fellowships that are reaching out to the lost. This does not include the parachurch ministries and hundreds of individual ministers who are hosting some kind of Christian fellowship, doing their part in the Gospel work.

In the last ten years, many churches have been growing steadily through the grace of God. The bigger churches are growing bigger, and many of the smaller churches are becoming smaller.

Many bigger churches are expanding their outreaches on the city island by building satellite sister churches. They've got the money, the people, and the resources to minister effectively to the communities. But the pastors of smaller churches suffer when their members give up and go to bigger, thriving churches. The members of smaller churches get discouraged and tired of "fighting" the good fight. When the members leave, the pastor is forced to close the church. Then what happens to his family?

Some of my pastor friends have said that Singapore is becoming the itinerants' graveyard. There are not many churches interested in either supporting or nurturing these itinerants. After a while, many of the traveling ministers become discouraged, pack their bags, and leave the ministry.

---

[51] http://www.omf.org.uk/content.asp?id=8519&cachefixer=.

Some ministers' wives have never worked throughout their married life as they were supported through his ministry. When the husband passes on, the wife is left without support as she goes back to work to support the family. Some ministers build their ministries on their personal anointing only without investing their life in others through mentorship. Ministry will experience different seasons of grace. When you are out of season for public ministry, continue a quiet ministry through a season of reaching out to the lost and building the Church. If you are not called to be a pastor, then find an apostolic leader who will embrace you and your family.

Be under the spiritual covering and continue your ministry. In this way, the children will grow in the grace of God rather than in bitterness of abandonment. I had assisted a few ministers' families when they experienced an impasse in these types of transitions.

There are many itinerant prophetic ministers who want to minister in churches, but they themselves and their families are not part of any church or accountable to anyone (Ephesians 4:16; Colossians 2:18,19).

I do not have the answers for all that is happening. But one thing is for certain: We must press on toward the mark of the Lord Jesus Christ. Go on all the way till the last drop of your blood is shed, in believing and serving the One who called you, knowing that God is faithful to those who will hang on with Him.

A PARADOX LIFE

Yes, there are times when God allows paradoxes in the lives of His servants as part of their spiritual grooming. As one who is called by the Lord, you will have the opportunity not only to experience the victories of Jesus, but also to walk through the wilderness. The Holy Spirit will prepare you for both seasons ahead of time, showing you how not to lose your head in pride during times of victory and how not to lose your spirit during times of discouragement.

Look at the example of Jesus, our Lord:

LUKE 4:1–2 AMPC

Then Jesus, full of and controlled by the Holy Spirit, returned from the Jordan and was led in [by] the [Holy] Spirit for (during) forty days in the wilderness (desert), where He was tempted (tried, tested exceedingly) by the devil. And He ate nothing during those days, and when they were completed, He was hungry.

When you meditate on the life of Jesus on the earth, you will witness firsthand His humanity, as well as His total dependence upon the Father for ministry direction (John 5:19–20), strength (Luke 22:43), and sermon outlines (John 7:16). Everything He did was through obedience to the Father's will for His life (John 4:34; 6:38).

I marvel at the life of Jesus—the way He prayed, the way He spoke of the Father, the way He conducted His ministry, His knowledge of the will of God at every turn of His life, and how He answered people's questions.

But at the same time, I wonder, with all of the power and angelic assistance (Matthew 26:53) He had, why did Jesus have to hide from the religious leaders at times?

JOHN 7:1–2 NKJV

After these things Jesus walked in Galilee; for He did not want to walk in Judea, because the Jews sought to kill Him.

JOHN 10:39

Again they tried to seize him, but he escaped their grasp.

Imagine what the disciples would have felt at these times. They saw a leader who talked "big" and yet "ran" and "hid." But that was not the case with our dear Lord! And this is the lesson I want to share with you.

THE TIMING OF GOD

PSALM 31:15 NKJV

My times are in Your hand; deliver me from the hand of my enemies, and from those who persecute me.

Our Lord Jesus had a "divine addiction" to do only the Father's will. He did only what He saw the Father doing. Here are some aspects of the life and ministry of our Lord Jesus to which all of us should adhere.

1. Jesus desired only to do the Father's will, nothing more and nothing less.

JOHN 4:34 AMPC

Jesus said to them, My food (nourishment) is to do the will (pleasure) of Him Who sent Me and to accomplish and completely finish His work.

JOHN 5:30 AMPC

I am able to do nothing from Myself [independently, of My own accord—but only as I am taught by God and as I get His orders]. Even as I hear, I judge [I decide as I am bidden to decide. As the voice comes to Me, so I give a decision], and My judgment is right (just, righteous), because I do not seek or consult My own will [I have no desire to do what is pleasing to Myself, My own aim, My own purpose] but only the will and pleasure of the Father Who sent Me.

2. Jesus' teaching was from the Father's heart and wisdom.

JOHN 8:28–29 AMPC

So Jesus added, When you have lifted up the Son of Man [on the cross], you will realize (know, understand) that I am He [for Whom you look] and that I do nothing of Myself (of My own accord or on My own authority), but I say [exactly] what My Father has taught Me. And He Who sent Me is ever with Me; My Father has not left Me alone, for I always do what pleases Him.

JOHN 14:10 AMPC

Do you not believe that I am in the Father, and that the Father is in Me? What I am telling you I do not say on My own authority and of My own accord; but the Father Who lives continually in Me does the (His) works (His own miracles, deeds of power).

3. Jesus' ministry reflected the Father's will for Him.

JOHN 5:36 AMPC

But I have as My witness something greater (weightier, higher, better) than that of John; for the works that the Father has appointed Me to accomplish and finish, the very same works that I am now doing, are a witness and proof that the Father has sent Me.

JOHN 9:4 AMPC

We must work the works of Him Who sent Me and be busy with His business while it is daylight; night is coming on, when no man can work.

4. The twelve disciples were the choice of the Father's will.

MARK 3:13–14 NKJV

And He went up on the mountain and called to Him those He Himself wanted. And they came to Him.

Then He appointed twelve, that they might be with Him and that He might send them out to preach.

JOHN 15:16 NKJV

You did not choose Me, but I chose you and appointed you that you should go and bear fruit, and that your fruit should remain, that whatever you ask the Father in My name He may give you.

What an example of divine timing in the life of Jesus! That is the example He has left for each one of us to follow.

JOHN 13:15 NKJV

For I have given you an example, that you should do as I have done to you.

1 PETER 2:21 NKJV

For to this you were called, because Christ also suffered for us, leaving us an example, that you should follow His steps.

1 JOHN 2:6 AMPC

Whoever says he abides in Him ought [as a personal debt] to walk and conduct himself in the same way in which He walked and conducted Himself.

The Lord Jesus has left behind examples for us, which ministers must reflect upon in order to walk under the divine timing of God. We are not to outshine others but to shine as bright as possible according to the grace that has been given to us (Romans 12:3).

Though Jesus operated in such a divine timing and strength, there were moments of frustration in His life, too. The Bible says:

- Jesus was in distress to finish the will of God (Luke 12:50).
- Jesus tolerated unbelief and others' lack of faith in His ministry (Matthew 17:17).
- Jesus became angry as He was deeply disturbed by the hardened hearts of people (Mark 3:5).
- Jesus displayed much sorrow and was troubled in heart, possibly while thinking of the sufferings that awaited Him (Matthew 26:37).
- Jesus wanted the company of three of His closest disciples, His friends, at the most crucial time of His life when He faced loneliness (Matthew 26:36–40).

Regardless of how spiritual we are, we will be allowed by God to walk through moments of sorrow and discouragement. Don't listen to the lies of the devil that you are going through these moments of discouragement because you are not spiritual enough or because the Father God is displeased with you. Jesus will never let go of you.

UNDERSTANDING SPIRITUAL WEARINESS

DANIEL 7:25 AMPC

And he shall speak words against the Most High [God] and shall wear out the saints of the Most High and think to change the time [of sacred feasts and holy days] and the law; and the saints shall be given into his hand for a time, two times, and half a time [three and one-half years].

The phrase "wear out" comes from the Aramaic word *bela*, meaning "to afflict one mentally and to harass one constantly." The satanic strategy of the end times is to wear out the saints. Once the spirit of discouragement is given permission to stay longer in your soul, it will affect the timing of your walk with God.

Many discouraged saints who have walked far away from God choose to walk in their own set of laws and in their own set of times and seasons. The will of God is the furthest thing from their hearts, as their spirits are too weak to pick up the stirrings of the Holy Spirit.

This is what the devil wants to achieve: to place the saints at the wrong time, with the wrong people, doing the wrong thing, and thereby sinning against God. Unless they repent, everything about their life goes downward without Jesus, just as it did for Jonah.

Child of God, are you the type who likes to think persistently about your past? Are you the type who would rather live in the past than look forward to the blessings of God for the future? Are you the type who wants everyone around you to listen to your stories rather than listen to the right counsel on how to get out of your past?

If you answered "yes" to all the above, then without any apology, I would like to tell you that you are the devil's favorite playground. The longer you choose to deny the grace of God to lift you up, to release your memories from the past, and to bring emotional healing to your soul, the greater of a fun ride the devil will have in your mind. You will then become bitter, wounded, and angry with yourself and others around you. Instead of fighting the devil off, you will tend to fight the very people God sends to rescue you out of your situation.

PSALM 107:14–15

He brought them out of darkness and the deepest gloom and broke away their chains. Let them give thanks to the LORD for his unfailing love and his wonderful deeds for men.

2 CORINTHIANS 4:6

For God, who said, "Let light shine out of darkness," made his light shine in our hearts to give us the light of the knowledge of the glory of God in the face of Christ.

ISAIAH 61:3 AMPC

To grant [consolation and joy] to those who mourn in Zion—to give them an ornament (a garland or diadem) of beauty instead of ashes, the oil of joy instead of mourning, the garment [expressive] of praise instead of a heavy, burdened, and failing spirit—that they may be called oaks of righteousness [lofty, strong, and magnificent, distinguished for uprightness, justice, and right standing with God], the planting of the Lord, that He may be glorified.

When you deny the power of God, refusing to let it touch you to bring the joy of the Lord into your life, you are a silent witness of the devil to the people around you—telling them that, after all, Jesus is not as powerful as people say He is. Child of God, rise up in the name of Jesus. Be all that God has called you to be.

When weariness sets in, handle it in prayer. The longer you choose to stay discouraged, the more your walk with God will slow down. Without your knowledge, you will lag behind in the call of God, and you will become a prime target for the enemy.

DEUTERONOMY 25:17–19

Remember what the Amalekites did to you along the way when you came out of Egypt. When you were weary and worn out, they met you on your journey and cut off all who were lagging behind; they had no fear of God. When the Lord your God gives you rest from all the enemies around you in the land he is giving you to possess as an inheritance, you shall blot out the memory of Amalek from under heaven. Do not forget!

The Lord Jesus wants to empower you to blot out the hurtful memories of your past from your soul. You have been lagging for far too long already. You are a soldier called to stand and fight for Him.

DANIEL 12:3

Those who are wise will shine like the brightness of the heavens, and those who lead many to righteousness, like the stars for ever and ever.

Maybe you are saying, "Lord, I don't want to be a servant or be in some sort of ministry. I just want to be a child of God and attend church." Let me tell you something I have been there, done that, too. Now, I know these are the words of a saint who is too weak in the spirit and who is just worn out. The brightness of their spirit is fading away. Yet Jesus came and revived and recommissioned me.

Jesus loves you so much that He has planned for you to shine like the brightness of the heavens and like the bright stars that help to navigate ships. He desires you to serve Him by leading many into righteousness! Hallelujah! He loves you. Live up to that!

It is time that we minister to the wounded saints and fainting soldiers.

ENTRY POINTS OF WEARINESS

There are some easy entry points of this spirit of weariness that you must look out for. The Bible says, "He that diggeth a pit shall fall into it; and whoso breaketh an hedge, a serpent shall bite him" (Ecclesiastes 10:8 KJV).

Beloved, when the walls of your life in Christ break down, the serpent will come in and bite. Your only security is to walk right in Christ and be protected in His name.

1. WHEN THE JOB IS TOO BIG FOR YOU

EXODUS 18:18 AMPC

You will surely wear out both yourself and this people with you, for the thing is too heavy for you; you are not able to perform it all by yourself.

Some people have a habit of wanting to be with everyone and being everywhere doing everything. They may think that they are being helpful, but when they check deep down in their hearts, it can possibly be an issue of hidden pride for attention. They may want their names to be mentioned in all things, always. It is highly possible that such people have misplaced priorities.

Moses was in a dilemma in his ministry. Leading the Israelites was fast becoming far too costly for him spiritually, emotionally, and physically. The Lord used his father-in-law to advise him and set him free from that weariness.

When the job you are doing is bigger than you are, frustration enters, and weariness follows.

2. SIN BRINGS WEARINESS TO THE SPIRIT MAN

JEREMIAH 9:5

Friend deceives friend, and no one speaks the truth. They have taught their tongues to lie; they weary themselves with sinning.

Deal with any known disobedience, and the Holy Spirit will reveal to you the hidden sins in your soul. Sin brings a heaviness in your heart that will prevent you from being able to move forward in the will of God and the path the Lord has laid before you.

PSALM 32:4–5

For day and night your hand was heavy upon me; my strength was sapped as in the heat of summer. Selah

Then I acknowledged my sin to you and did not cover up my iniquity. I said, "I will confess my transgressions to the LORD"—and you forgave the guilt of my sin.

The spirit of weariness in the form of depression is a direct satanic attack on your soul. Come under the blood of Jesus, confess your sins, and be lifted up in Jesus' name! (1 Peter 1:19).

3. DELAYED OBEDIENCE AND PROCRASTINATION BRINGS WEARINESS TO YOUR SOUL

JEREMIAH 20:9 AMPC

If I say, I will not make mention of [the Lord] or speak any more in His name, in my mind and heart it is as if there were a burning fire shut up in my bones. And I am weary of enduring and holding it in; I cannot [contain it any longer].

Jeremiah tried keeping the flow of the Spirit within his heart. Sometimes it frustrates you when you try to be the good guy and refuse to release the Word of the Lord. I know of some good-hearted pastor friends who would invite me to their church but would not want me to release the Word of the Lord. You cannot invite a prophet to your church and tell him not to prophesy. The Word of the Lord will be like fire in his bones. Weariness and frustration result when the Word of the Lord is denied its right passage of way.

Some of my minister friends are very frustrated in their present ministry. When you spend time with them, the issues that surface have always been the "doing"—thereby compromising the directives of the Lord. They often feel that they are doing something else, deviating from what God has called them to do.

God is not obligated to anoint you in any area in which He has not called you to minister. Sometimes you must just say no to nice and good suggestions and instead obey the primary objective the Lord has given you.

Beloved soldier, make sure you are with the right battalion, fighting the right battle given to you. The Holy Spirit gives the objectives for the mission. The Spirit of God will update you as you obediently complete each stage and phase. When you feel nothing is happening, don't turn back. Keep moving forward until the Word of the Lord comes to you.

4. SPIRITUAL BURDEN BRINGS WEARINESS TO YOUR SOUL

EZEKIEL 3:14 AMPC

So the Spirit lifted me up and took me away [in the vision], and I went in bitterness [of discouragement] in the heat of my spirit; and the hand of the Lord was strong upon me.

There are times when God will ask you to do projects that are bigger than your faith and vision. There will always be the expansion the Lord desires to bring in your life. But the choice is up to you as to whether you want to keep flowing with the Lord's vision at every stage or give up at some point and retire.

God is faithful. He will see you through. When He gives you a project, it could be bigger than what you have done before, but it is never bigger than the ability of God. Come to Him for His guidance. He will place the right people in your path to fulfill the Father's will.

The Apostle Paul cried in 2 Corinthians 11:28 ESV, "And, apart from other things, there is the daily pressure on me of my anxiety for all the churches." The word "anxiety" comes from the Greek word *merimno*, which means distraction. This is also the apostolic burden God will allow us to bear as part of spiritual grooming. You need to grow through these spiritual birth pangs to get the answers from the Lord.

There is no ministry without burden. We carry the burden of the churches under our spiritual care. You carry a spiritual burden for the pastors you love and care about. You bring them before the Throne of God for heavenly counsels. Such has been my experience. The Lord released His burden of His churches in my heart. The burden of my minister friends and the challenges they faced bears heavy on my soul.

I fast and pray for them. The Lord will reveal to me His counsels for them. This is a price to become His prophet. Carry the burden of the Lord, and He will use you as His mouthpiece. In my interaction with many pastors, I see an important dividing factor—the passion and burden for the work of the Lord. Many carry a professional opinion about their ministry and flock but not a spiritual passion. There is the other group, genuine shepherds who carry a compassion for the flock of God and a continued passion for the work of the ministry.

The burden of the Lord does not bury you. It will show you the path of intercession to the Throne of God. The door of revelation will be open to you. The prophet is called to be an intercessor before the mercy seat of heaven.

5. PHYSICAL AND SPIRITUAL FATIGUE BRINGS WEARINESS TO YOUR BODY AND SOUL

2 SAMUEL 17:1–2

Ahithophel said to Absalom, "I would choose twelve thousand men and set out tonight in pursuit of David. I would attack him while he is weary and weak. I would strike him with terror, and then all the people with him will flee."

When you break the laws of the natural body and push it beyond its limits, fatigue will force your body to seek rest. This is just simple common sense and the outworking of natural laws.

Just like Ahithophel's plan to attack David while he was weary and weak, the devil brings his smart bombs at the most vulnerable times in our lives. At times, it comes right after a time of ministry. When the anointing is lifted, you are just like anybody else. Manage your physical and spiritual wellness with wisdom.

Sometimes, my physical body would scream for rest and more sleep during long ministry trips. Yet I would push my body to wake up and pray a little longer. The Lord Jesus, during those moments, has been very gracious to let me rest. The strength of my spirit would still be at optimum level. Many times, I have felt the tangible anointing of the Holy Spirit flowing out of my palms. I believe it was to assure me that His grace is sufficient.

After a time of divine rest, your spirit is even sharper to respond to the leading of the Holy Spirit. In some meetings, I may have to pray for a few hundred people for hours. The Lord's kindness and goodness allows us to recover from spiritual fatigue.

ARE YOU JUST TIRED?

"The physiological effects of tiredness are well-known. You can turn a smart person into an idiot just by overworking him," notes Peter Capelli, a professor of management at Wharton.

THE MULTITASKING TRAP[52]

It's not really news that so-called multitasking can actually make people less effective at their jobs. One detailed study five years ago by psychologists at the University of Michigan demonstrated that, because the human brain needs time to shift gears between tasks, the more switching back and forth you have to do—say, talking on the phone, reading email, and thinking about your next meeting, all while eating a sandwich—the less proficiently you will tackle any of it (except maybe the sandwich). The "time cost" of refocusing your attention may be only a few seconds with each switch, but researchers found that, over time, it reduced people's total efficiency by 20 to 40 percent.

SPIRITUAL ANTIDOTE FOR RECOVERY

"You will have times of spiritual dryness. It is part of the Lord's way. But the fact you will have spiritual dry spells is not the issue.

---

[52] http://money.cnn.com/2006/03/16/news/economy/annie/fortune_annie 0317/index.htm.

The important question is, what you will do in a time of spiritual dryness? At this point, you must learn something about your natural tendencies. It will be the natural thing for you, during a dry season, to try to prove your love to the Lord. During a spiritually dry season you will find that you will try to prove to the Lord your faithfulness toward Him; you will do this by exerting your strength. Unconsciously you will be hoping by such self-effort to persuade Him to return more quickly."

"Do not be impatient in times of dryness and darkness; allow the removals and delays of the consolations of God; draw near to Him and wait upon Him patiently that your life may be increased and be renewed. So, dear children of the Lord, be patient in your prayer during those seasons of dryness," wrote Jeanne Guyon.[53]

PSALM 23:2–3 AMPC

He makes me lie down in [fresh, tender] green pastures; He leads me beside the still and restful waters. He refreshes and restores my life (my self); He leads me in the paths of righteousness [uprightness and right standing with Him—not for my earning it, but] for His name's sake.

JEREMIAH 31:25 AMPC

For I will [fully] satisfy the weary soul, and I will replenish every languishing and sorrowful person.

---

[53] Jeanne Guyon, *Experiencing the Depths of Jesus Christ* (Georgia: SeedSowers, MCMLXXV), 28–29.

MATTHEW 11:28 AMPC

Come to Me, all you who labor and are heavy-laden and overburdened, and I will cause you to rest. [I will ease and relieve and refresh your souls.]

It is the absolute will of God that we are refreshed and strengthened in our spirits, souls, and bodies to serve Him. Tired soldiers are no good for war. Not only they cannot defend themselves, but they will not be able to defend their fellow soldiers.

God has made His grace, mercy, and strength available for those who believe. Quit trying to serve Him in the flesh. You may desperately fail. Humble yourself in holy adoration to God on your knees, with hands lifted up, and surrender yourself. He will come and lift you up. The Bible reveals some scriptural ways to recover from this weariness.

1. GET BACK TO THE WORD OF GOD

PSALM 119:28 AMPC

My life dissolves and weeps itself away for heaviness; raise me up and strengthen me according to [the promises of] Your word.

The moment the Word of God is neglected through busyness in the ministry or any other affairs, you are on the verge of drying up your roots in Him. There is a famous quote that says, "Seven days without the Word makes one weak."

COLOSSIANS 2:7 AMPC

Have the roots [of your being] firmly and deeply planted [in Him, fixed and founded in Him], being continually built up in Him, becoming increasingly more confirmed and established in the faith, just as you were taught, and abounding and overflowing in it with thanksgiving.

The Word of God is the power source of heaven. Read it, study it, enjoy it, and live by it. There is an anointing that comes when you meditate on Jesus, who is the Word (John 1:1). He is the living Manna from heaven (John 6:35).

Dr. John Piper wrote, "Discipline and spontaneity. We need both in reading the Bible: discipline to move steadily through the books of the Bible, and spontaneity to go to a part of the Bible that we sense will meet a particular need. Both can be powerful with encouragement for faith. Sometimes in the midst of discipline, unexpected power will spring forth, and the line between spontaneity and discipline disappears."[54]

I want to share with you from my reflective journal:

> "My soul is greatly humbled when I stand before the Word. No matter how lousy or sinful I can feel before I touched this Book, after spending some time, I feel clean (Jn. 15:3), washed by the blood of Jesus (1 Jn. 1:9), sanctified by His Spirit, and strengthened by His Word (Rom. 15:16; 1 Co. 6:11).

---

[54] John Piper, *A Godward Life* (Sisters, OR: Multnomah, 1997), 56.

"I accepted Christ when I was fifteen years old. Through the constant discipling of my brother and a strong desire and hunger for the Word of Life, I poured my heart into the Word, often meditating for hours each day. The Word became the very air that I breathed.

"There was a total reconstruction of my inner self through His Word, although I am still a person 'under progress.' I love the Word. I surrender myself to the Word. There can be no voice, no opinion, no feeling that can stand against the Word.

"When I was twenty-one years of age, one of my friends asked me one evening why I quoted the Scriptures all the time. Without thinking twice, my tongue answered, 'Even if you would cut my veins, my blood will speak of the Word.' I was surprised by my quick answer. It was not meant to put him down, but it was because I knew for myself the depth of my devotion to Jesus and His Word.

"Fifteen years later, I read an excellent book, *A Godward Life* by Dr. John Piper, recommended by a God-given friend, Dr. Ajith Fernando. In the book, C.H. Spurgeon said of John Bunyan, 'Prick him anywhere; and you will find that his blood is Bibline, the very essence of the Bible flows from him. He cannot speak without a text, for his soul is full of the Word of God.'

"Oh, how much more I need to soak myself in His Words of life. My prayer and careful quest for these twenty-one years is that the Bible will not become a textbook from which I draw my sermons, but rather that the Bible will remain as God's revelation to me, and by meditating on it I will be changed and transformed by His image, a mark that I am far from and striving forward by the grace of God to become."

Every time I neglect the Word of God, I can feel the power of God draining from me. But when I spend time with the Lord, my cup runs over, and I feel fresh once again. Get back to the Word.

2. WAITING UPON THE LORD IN PRAYER

"You can work without praying, but it is a bad plan; but you cannot pray in earnest without working. Do not be so busy with work for Christ that you have no strength left for praying. True prayer requires strength."

—Hudson Taylor

ISAIAH 40:29–31 AMPC

He gives power to the faint and weary, and to him who has no might He increases strength [causing it to multiply and making it to abound]. Even youths shall faint and be weary, and [selected] young men shall feebly stumble and fall exhausted; but those who wait for the Lord [who expect, look for, and hope in Him] shall change and renew their strength and power; they shall lift their wings and mount up [close to God] as eagles [mount up to the sun];

they shall run and not be weary, they shall walk and not faint or become tired.

The first sign of self-surrender is when you take the time to wait upon the Lord. This is the altar on which you must die to the importance of self. Speaking of the importance of silence in waiting upon God, Henri Nouwen wrote, "It is not so strange that many ministers have become burnt-out cases, people who say many words and share many experiences, but in whom the fire of God's Spirit has died and from whom not much comes forth than their own boring, petty ideas and feelings."[55]

"Our first and foremost task is faithfully to care for the inward fire so that when it is really needed it can offer warmth and light to lost travelers."[56]

As we wait upon the Lord in prayer, by our actions, we are saying to the Lord, "You are more important to me than ministry, Lord!" I remember once when I was in deep prayer and waiting before God, I asked the Lord, "What is the ministry you want me to do, Lord?" to which the Lord replied in a crystal-clear voice, "My ministry is you—that the Father's purposes will be accomplished in your life!" Tears welled up, and I then understood the Father's love for each one of us.

He is not using us as puppets to do work for Him, but rather by loving Him and serving Him, the Holy Spirit desires to bring

---

[55] Henri J. M. Nouwen, *The Way of the Heart: Desert Spirituality and Contemporary Ministry* (HarperCollins, 1981), 54.

[56] Ibid., 55.

us into the conformation of His will and the transformation of our lives to become Christlike. That is the greatest pleasure of the Father (Romans 8:29; 2 Corinthians 3:18; Ephesians 4:24; 1 John 3:2).

"Time waiting on God in prayer is never lost. From your perspective there may be much waiting and apparent delay. From God's perspective your waiting in extended prayer is investment."[57]

As we learn to wait upon the Lord, the Holy Spirit sharpens our spiritual sensitivity to hear His voice and discern His directions. Do not make major decisions in life and ministry without fasting and praying before the Lord. Usually, in extended times of prayer, the Holy Spirit will guide you on how to wait upon the Lord.

ISAIAH 50:4–5 NASB

The Lord GOD has given Me the tongue of disciples, that I may know how to sustain the weary one with a word. He awakens Me morning by morning, He awakens My ear to listen as a disciple.

The Lord GOD has opened My ear; and I was not disobedient nor did I turn back.

My brother, Sadhu Sundar Selvaraj, is a man of prayer who fasts and waits upon God. He has been waking up at two in the morning and praying for hours for the past thirty years. The Lord has graced him with many spiritual experiences, and recently he

[57] Wesley L Duewel, *Let God Guide You Daily* (London: Marshall Pickering, 1988), 75.

taught on this subject of waiting on God in prayer. I encourage you to get this teaching and learn from people who practice the art of silence before God.

3. OPERATE IN THE GRACE AND MERCY OF GOD

2 CORINTHIANS 4:1 AMPC

Therefore, since we do hold and engage in this ministry by the mercy of God [granting us favor, benefits, opportunities, and especially salvation], we do not get discouraged (spiritless and despondent with fear) or become faint with weariness and exhaustion.

In all that God wants for you to be and do, live your life by the mercy of God. The mercy of God will keep you strong from spiritual exhaustion.

In February 2001, I conducted our first Rivers Ministers' Conference in Solo, Indonesia. Our ministry sponsored about four hundred pastors and their wives to come for the two-nights and three-days camp. I was the only speaker. The power of God was electrifying as the Lord touched each person through the Word of God.

When I came back to the hotel from the third session of the first day of the conference, my body was totally exhausted. Suddenly, I felt as if I had no message to share with the four hundred people. I felt as though heaven had just withdrawn all the anointing.

I did not know that it was a "setup." The Lord was about to teach me something from His Word. He made me feel the desperation of a minister without the grace of God, and through this, He showed me how dependent on Him we must become.

All the operations of our life in Christ are to be based on the grace of God. The Apostle Paul was such a man who lived and breathed the grace of God. Paul said the strength of God came upon him through the grace that flowed out superabundantly and beyond measure from Jesus Christ.

> **1 TIMOTHY 1:12, 14 AMPC**
>
> *I give thanks to Him Who has granted me [the needed] strength and made me able [for this], Christ Jesus our Lord, because He has judged and counted me faithful and trustworthy, appointing me to [this stewardship of] the ministry.*
>
> *And the grace (unmerited favor and blessing) of our Lord [actually] flowed out superabundantly and beyond measure for me, accompanied by faith and love that are [to be realized] in Christ Jesus.*

No wonder Paul was able to say in Philippians 4:13, "I have strength for all things in Christ Who empowers me [I am ready for anything and equal to anything through Him Who infuses inner strength into me; I am self-sufficient in Christ's sufficiency]" (AMPC).

The Lord has taught me how to depend more and more on the grace and strength that comes from Him spontaneously as I lean totally on Him. No matter how much we pray, fast, study the Word, and prepare spiritually for any ministry, heaven responds by the grace of God.

Beloved, through the grace of God, He has made us more than conquerors in Him (Romans 8:37). God has commanded strength to be made available to each one of us.

OPS BRIEFING 5

SATANIC STRONGHOLDS OVER NATIONS

DANIEL 10:10–14 NLT

Just then a hand touched me and lifted me, still trembling, to my hands and knees.

And the man said to me, "Daniel, you are very precious to God, so listen carefully to what I have to say to you. Stand up, for I have been sent to you." When he said this to me, I stood up, still trembling. Then he said, "Don't be afraid, Daniel. Since the first day you began to pray for understanding and to humble yourself before your God, your request has been heard in heaven. I have come in answer to your prayer.

But for twenty-one days the spirit prince of the kingdom of Persia blocked my way. Then Michael, one of the archangels, came to help me, and I left him there with the spirit

> *prince of the kingdom of Persia. Now I am here to explain what will happen to your people in the future, for this vision concerns a time yet to come.*

I was only seventeen years old, but I was ready to serve God. During my school holidays, I decided to go and preach the Gospel to my relatives in Malaysia. In my early years of serving God, I had no one to talk to; no one knew me as a minister, and I had no ministry credentials. I would just soak myself in the Lord for about four hours each day and seven hours each weekend, praying and meditating on the Scriptures.

In one of these mini mission trips to Malaysia, I went to a cousin's house so that we could pray together. Within a week, about thirty people gathered in the house for prayer as the Holy Spirit fell upon them. Many were healed and delivered by the power of God. Many experienced healing from sicknesses.

One afternoon, I went to have a shower. In the bathroom, as I closed my eyes to pour a small bucket of water over my head, I saw in an open vision a strong female demon spirit. It stood outside the bathroom and looked straight into my eyes. Suddenly a spirit of fear gripped me, which I could not understand.

As fear gripped me, I quickly left the bathroom to my room. This high-ranking demonic spirit stood outside the room and looked at me from the windows, and stared at me to further infuse fear. At this point, I was getting ready for a house prayer meeting in a remote village. The fear infused by the spirit wanted me to cancel the meeting.

About four hours later, on the way to the meeting place, which was in a remote village, the residents told me that they worshiped this demon as their goddess. She was the ruling spirit of that village. Only then did I realize that this demon had come to deter me from preaching the Gospel in her territory.

In that meeting, the Lord Jesus manifested His power in such a mighty way. There were salvations of souls, healings of spine problems and kidney problems, and deliverances from demonic powers. The Lord Jesus' name was exalted.

The ability to see the controlling spirits of territories has become a regular occurrence in my ministry. The Lord reveals the hidden strongholds to me, so that as His prophet, I can be effective for His Kingdom and demonstrate His power. I have seen the spirits of witches who constantly cast spells of control over certain towns in Australia, and I have seen the spirit of Jezebel many times.

SATAN'S INFLUENCE ON THE EARTH

Speaking of the devil, E.M. Bounds wrote, "He is not only the source of evil to others, but the embodiment of evil in a person."[58]

On August 7, 2005, a Sunday morning, the Holy Spirit filled me with His anointing and poured His wisdom into my heart. He revealed to me that satanic strongholds, like the prince of Persia mentioned in the book of Daniel, exercise certain rights of control in given regions. Their control extends even into the realms of politics, economics, education systems, culture, media, and business.

---

[58] E.M. Bounds, *Winning the Invisible War* (Whitaker House, 1984), 15.

These strongholds, or chief demon princes, of certain locations have control in establishing false apostles in politics and false prophets in the financial markets and in the wealth management of the nations. Through the influence of these strongholds, there will arise false evangelists, who will propagate anti-Christ and anti-law agendas to promote ungodliness; permissive lifestyles and sexual immorality will saturate all forms of media. There will be the rise of false teachers, who will spread satanic ideologies, and false pastors, who will nurture and breed the next level of leadership to continue the demonic system of world government and promote one-world governance.

The Lord then said that the Church must rise up in prevailing prayer and intercession to release the souls in bondage from all levels of society—including the souls of influential people, celebrities, and top government officials—into the Kingdom of God.

THE SPIRIT OF BABYLON

In November 2005, I was invited to minister at an Apostolic and Prophetic Intercession Seminar organized by a dear friend of mine, Reverend James Halliday of Mannahouse Ministries, NSW, Australia. I had prepared a different set of notes to teach to the seminar attendees.

On an early morning before the seminar, while I was in prayer, the Spirit of God showed me by revelation from the Word about the operations of the spirit of Babylon.

REVELATION 2:12–13

"To the angel of the church in Pergamum write: These are the words of him who has the sharp, double-edged sword. I know where you live—where Satan has his throne. Yet you remain true to my name. You did not renounce your faith in me, even in the days of Antipas, my faithful witness, who was put to death in your city—where Satan lives."

Jesus said, "I know where you live—where Satan has his throne." What a powerful, all-knowing God we serve! Jesus knows all about Satan and his activities. Jesus knows exactly where Satan has his base of operations, and it does not take long for Jesus to flush him out. Yet the Lord has given some time for all things (according to His divine plan) to take place before Satan is forever banished from the earth (Revelation 12:12; 20:10).

As the Second Coming of Jesus draws nigh, a powerful organization is being set up on this earth. Its politicians are empowered by the strong and powerful spirit of Babylon. The principal spirits in this satanic government will be the spirit of Jezebel, the spirit of Babylon, the Antichrist, and the false prophet. Each of these four spirits is mentioned in the book of Revelation. There has been a systematic build-up of their operations on this earth, which have been active for many years in different parts of the world.

"The devil is a hydra-headed monster that is multifaceted in plans and wisdom as well as in atrocities. His supreme effort is to get control of the Church, not to destroy its organization, but to pervert its divine purposes. He does this in the most insidious way with no startling change and nothing to shock or alarm,"[59] wrote E.M. Bounds.

COME OUT OF BABYLON!

ISAIAH 52:11

Depart, depart, go out from there! Touch no unclean thing! Come out from it and be pure, you who carry the vessels of the LORD.

REVELATION 18:4–5

Then I heard another voice from heaven say: "Come out of her, my people, so that you will not share in her sins, so that you will not receive any of her plagues; for her sins are piled up to heaven, and God has remembered her crimes."

The Holy Spirit is calling His people to come out from under the influence and the spirit of Babylon. The judgments of the Lord have begun upon the face of the earth. The prophets of the Old Testament—mentioned in Jeremiah 50:8; 51:6, 45—carried out this same prophetic admonition. God's people must separate themselves from that which is worldly and anti-God.

What exactly is the spirit of Babylon? This answer varies, depending on the many countries, cultures, and religions of the world. Anything that alienates you from walking with God must be confronted, whether it is from within your soul or from outside

---

[59] E.M. Bounds, *Winning the Invisible War* (Whitaker House, 1984), 40.

of you, in the world. Be like Babylon, and you are Babylon. If you share in her sins, then you will have a share in her judgments that come from the Throne of God.

And this judgment, my beloved, has already begun!

> **In my well-worn-out study Bible of twenty years, I pasted a simple quote in 1986: "Anything that dims my vision of Christ, or takes away my taste for Bible study, or cramps my prayer life, or makes Christian work difficult, is wrong for me, and I must, as a Christian, turn away from it."**
>
> —J.W. Chapman

The father of faith, Abraham, in obedience to divine direction, left the idolatrous city of Ur, modern-day Iraq, and made his way to the land of Israel. In this land, Abraham entered into a covenant relationship with the God of Israel (Genesis 12). In the same manner, today the Holy Spirit is drawing the people of God away from the spirit of Babylon and toward the spirit of righteousness.

Today's modern Iraq was known as Babylon in biblical times. Apart from Israel, Babylon is the most discussed nation in the Bible. If the city of Jerusalem is the city of God, then the city of Babylon can be identified as the city of Satan. The spirit of Babylon draws people to herself, as she is part of the kingdom of darkness.

Each one of us must walk according to the Scriptures and the leading of the Holy Spirit to determine whether we are walking in purity before the Lord (2 Corinthians 6:14–7:1). Dual citizenship with the world and with heaven is denied to the child of God. We have been delivered from the dominion of this world and transported into the Kingdom of Jesus, the Son of God (Ephesians 2:19; Philippians 3:20; Colossians 1:13).

THE SPIRIT OF JEZEBEL'S OPERATIONS

2 TIMOTHY 3:1 AMPC

But understand this, that in the last days will come (set in) perilous times of great stress and trouble [hard to deal with and hard to bear].

The word *perilous* here comes from the Greek word *chalepos*, which conveys the idea of reducing strength, making it difficult and dangerous. An interesting note about this Greek word is that it only appears twice in the New Testament. The other Scripture passage where this same Greek word appears is found in Matthew 8:28. The word *fierce* was used in the context of demon possession of the man who lived in a cemetery.

By putting these two verses together, we can gather that in the last days, the world will witness an increase in satanic activity involving demons of the highest order.

In my meetings, the Lord has shown me controlling demonic spirits that live in cemeteries. These are very powerful and territorial. Often, when these demons possess an individual, it requires a higher level of anointing to encounter a deliverance. A higher level of anointing manifests through prayer, fasting, and a consecrated life to God.

Though my experience is subjective, I have often heard of other deliverance ministers who relate similar experiences. In the Scriptures, the disciples of Jesus were dismayed that they were not able to handle a deaf and dumb spirit, but when Jesus gave the command, the spirit left. Jesus told His disciples, "This kind can come forth by nothing, but by prayer and fasting" (Mark 9:29 KJV). Our Lord Jesus lived in constant communion with the Father. His lifestyle of fasting kept the anointing of the Holy Spirit always at an optimum level.

Territorial spirits are stronger and are high-ranking in the demonic kingdom. When a church is planted in their area, it is vital that the minister is led by God, more than a simple "feeling of faith" to plant the work in a demonic area. It is the work of the church to clear the darkness so that the glory of God will manifest. When the church planter carries a prophetic anointing and is seasoned in the ministry, he will carry the wisdom of God to encounter the challenges, both demonic and natural, in the given area.

When the Lord Jesus sent me to plant a church in Shelby, North Carolina, such was the case. On the second day of our new purchase of the church property, while praying in the conference room, one of the youths in our prayer circle saw a demonic spirit standing outside and looking at us. When he said that, I turned around, and there it was—a black, dark demonic spirit that took the form of a young boy of about twelve years standing outside on each side of the room.

I stepped out to pray and cast these spirits out. My physical body felt the chills of a dark presence that was in control of this place. I spoke authoritatively in tongues and walked around the offices as I declared the holiness of God. When I stood outside one of the rooms, I saw in the spirit a noose was hanging. I told the demonic spirits to remove all their items and get out of this place. I told them; that this property belongs to Jesus My King now. After almost an hour of prayer, the atmosphere changed to peace.

Two demonic spirits speak of mischievous spirits. They create unnecessary troubles, and no one will be able to trace who started it. A noose represents the spirit of death that will cause the work of the Church to stop. One of the elders asked me, "How do we stop them?"

My answer, "Live a consecrated and holy life! Let us be accountable and conduct ourselves honorably with financial accountability. Do not give these spirits a reason to camp in the church. When they see the holiness of God, the demonic spirits will scatter."

The Church must teach the fullness of the Word and worship God in holiness. The people must walk in the Spirit and in love. The Church must focus on spiritual maturity so that there is maturity. We must conquer ground for Jesus and manifest the glory of God.

In the last days, there will be a powerful convergence of demonic strongholds to deter the work of God and the saints. The Antichrist, the false prophet, the spirit of Jezebel, and the spirit of Babylon will fiercely oppose the Body of Christ.

I want to briefly share with you the illumination the Spirit of God showed me one morning. My intention is to share the pointers given by the Holy Spirit rather than to provide a verse-by-verse commentary on the Scriptures here.

1. ATTACK ON THE MINISTERS OF GOD

REVELATION 2:20

Nevertheless, I have this against you: You tolerate that woman Jezebel, who calls herself a prophetess. By her teaching she misleads my servants into sexual immorality and the eating of food sacrificed to idols.

There will be a release of false teachings from the mind of this Jezebelic spirit meant to mislead the ministers of God. There will be a high-profile attack on the minds of ministers. Once these preachers of the Gospel are infected, they in turn will spread the false teachings to their congregations, and through various forms of media, to the world. The teachings will produce permissive lifestyles until there no longer is a dividing line between the holiness of God and the ungodliness of the world (1 Timothy 4:1–2; 2 Timothy 3:1–4; 2 Peter 2:1–3; 2 Corinthians 11:13–15; Galatians 2:4; Ephesians 4:14; Colossians 2:4; 2 Thessalonians 2:2; 1 Timothy 1:9; Titus 1:10–11; 1 John 2:26; 4:1). Ministers who have opened their hearts to the spirit of greed and covetousness are vulnerable to the work of this spirit.

Ministers who are not rooted in the Word and those who preach messages that lack the power of the Holy Spirit are susceptible to these misleadings of demonic spirits. We need to become rooted in His Word. Teach the meat of the Word to the congregation so that they mature in the Lord's image.

> **Colossians 2:7 AMPC**
>
> *Have the roots [of your being] firmly and deeply planted [in Him, fixed and founded in Him], being continually built up in Him, becoming increasingly more confirmed and established in the faith, just as you were taught, and abounding and overflowing in it with thanksgiving.*

2. THE SPIRIT OF NIMROD, THE REBELLIOUS

> **REVELATION 2:24**
>
> *Now I say to the rest of you in Thyatira, to you who do not hold to her teaching and have not learned Satan's so-called deep secrets (I will not impose any other burden on you).*

It is rather interesting to note the phrase here: "Satan's so-called deep secrets." What are these deep secrets? How can one study the secrets of the dark side? We must investigate the history of both the founder and the beginning of the Babylonian kingdom.

NIMROD, FOUNDER OF BABYLON

In the book of Genesis, we read of Nimrod as being the founder of the kingdom of Babylon (Genesis 10:8–9). In Micah 5:6, Babylon is designated as "the land of Nimrod." The name *Nimrod* in the

Hebrew means "rebel and revolt." The Bible states, "He [Nimrod] was a mighty hunter before the LORD" (Genesis 10:9).

According to Joseph Seiss, in his classic commentary *The Apocalypse*, "The Targum of Jonathan" interprets this expression this way: "Nimrod was a mighty rebel before the Lord, the mightiest rebel before the Lord that was ever in the earth." And "The Jerusalem Targum (Aramaic paraphrase of the Hebrew Bible)" states that "Nimrod was mighty in sin before the Lord, a hunter of the sons of men."

In the Bible, Nimrod appears as a great personality in whom earthly imperial power first appeared in human history. This evil character appears in several observations:

a. Earthly kingship initially came into existence among the Hamitic peoples, upon the branch of Noah's descendants on which a prophetic curse had been pronounced and in the entire family in which there was an absence of the divine blessing (Genesis 9:25–27).
b. Nimrod is represented as the establisher of Babylon (Genesis 10:8–12), which is invariably outlined in Scripture both in type and prophecy as a religiously and morally evil system (Isaiah 21:9; Jeremiah 50:24; 51:64; Revelation 16:19; 17:5; 18:2–3).
c. Nimrod's name "no doubt suggested to the Israelites the idea of 'rebelling' against God" (A. Dillmann, *Genesis* [1897], 1:350). The name Nimrod in the divine account is meant to suggest the concept of rebellion as descriptive of the character of this first-world empire-builder, despite the

fact that the original name in Hamitic speech did not have this meaning.

Nimrod is said to have been "a mighty hunter before the LORD" (Genesis 10:9). The simple meaning of this statement is that Nimrod was the exact opposite of the divine ideal of a kinglike shepherd (cf. 2 Samuel 5:2; 7:7; 1 Peter 5:4). A hunter gratifies himself at the expense of his victims, whereas a shepherd expends himself for the good of the subjects in his care. Nimrod has been connected with the legendary name of Gilgamesh, the demi-god-king of Uruk (biblical Erech, Genesis 10:10). Nimrod's designation as a "hunter" clearly connects him with the founding of a military state based on absolute power. However, Babylonian and Assyrian art picturing wild animals in hunting scenes may point to Nimrod also as a literal hunter, which, in the Hebrew account, is given a religious connotation.[60] Babylon, as a city, reached its glory at about 600 BC under the reign of King Nebuchadnezzar.

Through the building of the city of Babylon, Nimrod was attempting to build a one-world government, and through the Tower of Babel, he attempted to establish a one-world religion. Both satanic strategies are already in place in the earth and are drawing millions of people around the world.

---

60 *The New Unger's Bible Dictionary.* Originally published by Moody Press of Chicago, Illinois. Copyright (c) 1988.

THE MYSTERY RELIGION OF WITCHCRAFT AND SORCERY

Nimrod's wife, Semiramis, was acknowledged as the founder of the Babylonian mystery religions, and she was the first high priestess of this order. She was acknowledged as the "queen of heaven." This order had many secret rites, including idolatry and consecrated prostitution. Therefore she becomes a prototype of the woman mentioned in Revelation 17:1–5, with the words written on her forehead: "Mystery Babylon the Great, The Mother of Harlots and Abominations of the Earth."

Semiramis outlived Nimrod by forty-two years, and according to ancient historical documents, due to her loose and licentious living, she gave birth to a son after the death of Nimrod. She called him Tammuz, and he was worshiped as a savior of his people.

The legend of the mother and child was incorporated into the Babylonian religious rites and in other pagan religions.

The mother was pictured as the "queen of heaven" with the baby in her arms. These rites are practiced through the religions in Canaan, Egypt, Phoenicia, Assyria, Greece, and Rome. During the Dark Ages of church history, there was an infiltration of this mystery religion into Christianity.

Although the natural kingdom of Babylon has been destroyed, the spirit of Babylon lives on. The book of Revelation mentions the word *Babylon* six times:

REVELATION 14:8

A second angel followed and said, "Fallen! Fallen is Babylon the Great, which made all the nations drink the maddening wine of her adulteries."

REVELATION 16:19

The great city split into three parts, and the cities of the nations collapsed. God remembered Babylon the Great and gave her the cup filled with the wine of the fury of his wrath.

REVELATION 17:5

This title was written on her forehead: MYSTERY BABYLON THE GREAT THE MOTHER OF PROSTITUTES AND OF THE ABOMINATIONS OF THE EARTH.

REVELATION 18:2

With a mighty voice he shouted: "Fallen! Fallen is Babylon the Great! She has become a home for demons and a haunt for every evil spirit, a haunt for every unclean and detestable bird."

REVELATION 18:10

Terrified at her torment, they will stand far off and cry: "Woe! Woe, O great city, O Babylon, city of power! In one hour your doom has come!"

REVELATION 18:21

Then a mighty angel picked up a boulder the size of a large millstone and threw it into the sea, and said: "With such violence the great city of Babylon will be thrown down, never to be found again.

In Genesis 11, through Nimrod's influence, the people erected the Tower of Babel. The purpose for building this city was to centralize a singular kingdom. It was from this high tower that Nimrod observed and learned much of astrology, which is satanic in origin. The Lord came down and destroyed this tower that symbolized rebellion against God and His order. The spread of idol worship, witchcraft, sorcery, blood sacrifices, and other evil practices associated with the worship of Satan attracted the judgment of God.

But the question remains: How did Nimrod learn so much about witchcraft at that time? Some extrabiblical books, like the Book of Enoch, reveal that it was the fallen angels that taught the human race how to conduct satanic rituals and worship (Genesis 6:2, 4). This became the entry point for Satan and his cohorts to become directly involved in the affairs of the human race and to control and possess human beings themselves.

It is not difficult to understand the common sense of this approach, "Who then can teach anyone about the 'deep secrets of Satan' when none knew 'how to'?" It was the evil in the hearts (Genesis 6:5) of men that attracted such teachings of rebellion against the worship of the God of heaven, the Creator, Elohim.

A SOCIETY OF SELF-PLEASERS

In Revelation 18, the Apostle John reveals specific sins that the spirit of Babylon will perpetuate throughout the earth. The first is the spirit of idolatry, and the second is the spirit of pride, as mentioned in Revelation 18:7: "she glorified herself" (NKJV), thinking of herself as the queen who can never be dethroned (Isaiah 47:7–9). The third sin is the spirit of worldly pleasures and luxury (Revelation 18:7). The cult of self-empowerment by the spirits of greed and covetousness will drive people to become pleasers of self.

2 TIMOTHY 3:2–5 AMPC

For people will be lovers of self and [utterly] self-centered, lovers of money and aroused by an inordinate [greedy] desire for wealth, proud and arrogant and contemptuous boasters. They will be abusive (blasphemous, scoffing), disobedient to parents, ungrateful, unholy and profane.

[They will be] without natural [human] affection (callous and inhuman), relentless (admitting of no truce or appeasement); [they will be] slanderers (false accusers, troublemakers), intemperate and loose in morals and conduct, uncontrolled and fierce, haters of good. [They will be] treacherous [betrayers], rash, [and] inflated with self-conceit. [They will be] lovers of sensual pleasures and vain amusements more than and rather than lovers of God.

For [although] they hold a form of piety (true religion), they deny and reject and are strangers to the power of it

> *[their conduct belies the genuineness of their profession]. Avoid [all] such people [turn away from them].*

3. CONTROL OF WORLD POLITICS

REVELATION 18:3

> *For all the nations have drunk the maddening wine of her adulteries. The kings of the earth committed adultery with her, and the merchants of the earth grew rich from her excessive luxuries.*

There will be direct satanic influences that come upon many political leaders of various nations in order to legalize sin. The Bible says that "where sin abounded, grace abounded much more" (Romans 5:20 NKJV). When you legalize sin and suppress the grace of God (Romans 1:18), then sin attracts the judgment of God (Romans 1:21–32).

4. CONTROL OF WORLD ECONOMICS

REVELATION 18:3, 11–13

> *For all the nations have drunk the maddening wine of her adulteries. The kings of the earth committed adultery with her, and the merchants of the earth grew rich from her excessive luxuries. The merchants of the earth will weep and mourn over her because no one buys their cargoes any more—cargoes of gold, silver, precious stones and pearls; fine linen, purple, silk and scarlet cloth; every sort of citron*

wood, and articles of every kind made of ivory, costly wood, bronze, iron and marble; cargoes of cinnamon and spice, of incense, myrrh and frankincense, of wine and olive oil, of fine flour and wheat; cattle and sheep; horses and carriages; and bodies and souls of men.

REVELATION 18:23b

Your merchants were the world's great men. By your magic spell all the nations were led astray.

The spirit of Babylon will attract many investors toward herself. During the end times, Babylon will become the gold mine of investments.

- Oil: There is already a great interest in it, and there will be more so in the future as the oil-rich countries and Babylon will become the center of wealth management. The oil riches are possibly hinted at with the words, "as many as trade by sea" (Revelation 18:17 KJV).
- Investments: "merchandise of gold, and silver, and precious stones, and of pearls."
- Textiles: "fine linen, and purple and silk, and scarlet cloth."
- Building and construction materials: "every sort of citron wood, and articles of every kind made of ivory, costly wood, bronze, iron, and marbles."
- Luxury goods: "of cinnamon and spice, of incense, myrrh and frankincense."
- Food: "wine, and oil, and fine flour and wheat."

- Meat: "beasts, and sheep."
- Transportation: "horses, and chariots."
- Labor: "slaves and souls of men."

5. ESTABLISHMENT OF SPIRITUAL BABYLONIAN CULTURE

REVELATION 18:2

With a mighty voice he shouted: "Fallen! Fallen is Babylon the Great! She has become a home for demons and a haunt for every evil spirit, a haunt for every unclean and detestable bird."

REVELATION 18:22

The music of harpists and musicians, flute players and trumpeters, will never be heard in you again.

There will be the rise of a one-world religion through the establishment of a religious structure and order.

REVELATION 13:3–4, 8

One of the heads of the beast seemed to have had a fatal wound, but the fatal wound had been healed. The whole world was astonished and followed the beast. Men worshiped the dragon because he had given authority to the beast, and they also worshiped the beast and asked, "Who is like the beast? Who can make war against him?"

All inhabitants of the earth will worship the beast—all whose names have not been written in the book of life belonging to the Lamb that was slain from the creation of the world.

6. HER OBJECTIVE: OPPOSING THE SAINTS

REVELATION 18:20

Rejoice over her, O heaven! Rejoice, saints and apostles and prophets! God has judged her for the way she treated you.

REVELATION 18:24

In her was found the blood of prophets and of the saints, and of all who have been killed on the earth.

REVELATION 19:2

For true and just are his judgments. He has condemned the great prostitute who corrupted the earth by her adulteries. He has avenged on her the blood of his servants.

The Church must rise up in the power and the anointing of the Holy Spirit. She must continue to separate herself and her ways from the conduct of this world to show herself as separated unto the Lord. The victory that our Lord Jesus purchased for us must run through the veins of the Church. We are called to walk in triumphant victory in the name of Jesus over the works of darkness (2 Corinthians 2:14).

ISAIAH 52:11–12 TLB

Go now, leave your bonds and slavery. Put Babylon and all it represents far behind you—it is unclean to you. You are the holy people of the Lord; purify yourselves, all you who carry home the vessels of the Lord. You shall not leave in haste, running for your lives, for the LORD will go ahead of you, and he, the God of Israel, will protect you from behind.

JEREMIAH 51:6 NLT

Flee from Babylon! Save yourselves! Don't get trapped in her punishment! It is the LORD's time for vengeance; he will repay her in full.

2 CORINTHIANS 6:17 NLT

Therefore, come out from among unbelievers and separate yourselves from them, says the LORD. Don't touch their filthy things, and I will welcome you.

REVELATION 18:4–5 NLT

Then I heard another voice calling from heaven, "Come away from her, my people. Do not take part in her sins, or you will be punished with her. For her sins are piled as high as heaven, and God remembers her evil deeds."

THE EUROPEAN UNION IN BIBLE PROPHECY[61]

The most important prophetic development of the twentieth century was the regathering of the Jewish people to their historic homeland in the Middle East, resulting in the creation of the state of Israel on May 14, 1948. The second most important development was the formation of a European confederation known as the European Union. Both momentous historical events point to the fact that we are living in the end times, that we are right on the threshold of the Tribulation period and the Lord's return.

The Council of the Union is the chief legislative body for the EU. It is headquartered in Brussels, Belgium, and it consists of eighty-seven representatives appointed by the member states. Some decisions require a unanimous vote, but most only require a "qualified majority" of sixty-two votes. The voting is weighted in relation to the size of the countries.

The Parliament of the Union consists of 626 members who are directly elected for a five-year term. The Parliament is a parliament in name only. It is primarily a public forum whose members sit in blocs organized according to their political views rather than their nationalities.

The EU has been growing in power in recent years. The Parliament holds its committee meetings at a facility in Brussels; although, its plenary sessions are conducted at its elaborate new headquarters in Strasbourg, France. Although it has recently

---

61 Dr. David Reagan, "Europe in Bible Prophecy Introduction," article taken from https://lamblion.com/xfiles/publications/magazines/Lamplighter_MayJun01_EuropeanUnion.pdf

gained some "co-decision" power, its influence is felt primarily through its discussions and resolutions.

The Commission of the Union is the agency responsible for implementing legislation. It is the executive branch. There are twenty commissioners: two each from France, Germany, Italy, Spain, and Britain, and one from each of the other member states. Commissioners are appointed for five-year terms. The Commission's president is the chief executive officer of the European Union.

The Court of Justice has its headquarters in Luxembourg. There are fifteen justices, one from each member state, appointed for terms of six years. Judgments of the Court in the field of EU law are binding on all member states, their national courts, their companies, and their private citizens. The decisions override those of national courts.

The Central Bank is located in Frankfurt, Germany, and is responsible for monetary policy and the new Euro currency, which was introduced in January 1999 and replaced the member states' national currencies in 2002.

Revenue for the Union in 2000 came to $93.2 billion. The largest source of income was the 1.27 percent of gross national income that each member state was required to pay. In the year 2000, this levy produced 47.8 percent of the Union's revenue. The next highest source (36.4 percent) came from a 1 percent VAT tax (value-added tax) on goods and services. The rest of the income came from an assortment of agricultural levies and custom duties.

THE EMERGENCE OF A SUPERSTATE

The European Union is poised for a major expansion. In March 1998, the EU opened talks on full membership with six countries—Cyprus, Czech Republic, Estonia, Hungary, Poland, and Slovenia. In October 1999, the Commission proposed talks with another six—Bulgaria, Latvia, Lithuania, Malta, Romania, and Slovakia. When these countries are added, nearly all the people of Europe will be joined in a single Union by free and democratic consent for the first time in history.

The movement for European unity was launched in 1950 by Robert Schuman and Jean Monnet. This now has gradually evolved into a superstate. An official publication of the European Union states: "The EU system is inherently evolutionary. It was designed to allow for the gradual development of European unification and has not yet achieved its final form."[62]

The European Union now manifests three of the most important characteristics of a state. It has a unified economic system, an integrated political structure, and a shared vision for the future. Prophecy teacher Jimmy DeYoung points out that it even has a common language—namely English.[63] Although many languages

---

62 "The European Union: A Guide for Americans," published by the Delegation of the European Commission in the United States, Washington, D.C., October 1999, 7. This is an excellent booklet, and it can be obtained free of charge by writing The Delegation of The European Commission, 2300 M Street, NW, Washington, D.C. 20037. Or you can order it from the Delegation's website at www.eurunion.org.

63 Jimmy DeYoung, "Europe, NATO and the Antichrist," *Israel My Glory*, March/April 2001, 19.

are spoken by the member nations and their representatives, almost all know English because the internet has made it the common trade language.

What the Union officially lacks is a military force. But that is in the making. Military staff have been assembled, with a commander-in-chief appointed, and it currently has at its disposal sixty thousand frontline troops on standby, with four hundred assault aircrafts and up to eighty warships.[64] The British government refers to this as a "rapid reaction force." This is nothing but a euphemism for an "army." It has been dubbed "Eurocorps" by the rest of Europe, and it was supposed to be ready for action in 2003. The British are downplaying this military arm of the European Union because they want to continue their partnership with the United States in NATO. The French would like to see the Eurocorps replace NATO, and it probably will.

THE TOWER OF BABEL

Modeled on Pieter Bruegel's famous sixteenth-century painting, *The Tower of Babel,* the image shows the people of Europe rebuilding the tower that God destroyed in Genesis 11:5–9.

An amazing poster was issued by the European Union, showing the Tower of Babel and carrying the slogan: "Many Tongues, One Voice." In case the point was lost on the viewer, a crane in the

[64] *EU: Final World Empire,* a video program by Alan Franklin and Tony Pearce produced by Hearthstone and distributed in the USA by Southwest Radio Church in Oklahoma City, Oklahoma.

background was shown rebuilding the tower. Above the Tower of Babel was shown the Euro-stars, but they were inverted, as in witchcraft, with the central points facing downward. The story of the rise and fall of Babylon, told in Genesis 11, should have been a warning to all men for all time. Nimrod and his followers tried to build a tower to reach the heavens, but it was a counterfeit building of a counterfeit religion.

Mystical Babylon is now being rebuilt in Europe, and those who would follow Nimrod have now succeeded in building a parliament building in Strasbourg, France, whose centerpiece is an enormous replica of the unfinished Tower of Babel. Even the secular press could not miss the connection between the old and new towers of Babel. They labeled the new French structure *The Tower of Euro-Babel.* This monumental building, full of labyrinthine corridors, is used only one week out of four because the rest of the time, the EU Parliament meets in committees in Brussels. Every three weeks, the whole caboodle shuffles between the two sites in a fleet of two hundred trucks at enormous expense. A member of the European Parliament was there on the day Euro-Babel opened and reported total chaos in the £300 million structure, commenting: "If they can't run a building, should we trust them with a continent?"

Nigel Farage is a member of the European Parliament who belongs to the United Kingdom Independence Party, which is fighting to get Britain out of the superstate. He said in an article published just after the opening day: "We realize we are not merely entering a building, but we are being allowed access to the temple of a bold new empire."[65]

THE WOMAN RIDING A BEAST

On December 9, 1991, *Time* magazine showed a woman riding a bull while holding aloft the European flag, which is used to picture the European movement.

Another demonic biblical symbol that is being used in conjunction with the European Union is the one from Revelation 17, where a "great harlot" is depicted riding a beast. For some strange and unknown reason, this symbol is being used to represent the EU! For example, when Britain issued a stamp to commemorate the first European Parliament elections in 1979, the picture on the stamp depicted a woman riding a beast.

According to the Rev. Dr. Ian Paisley, a Northern Ireland Protestant minister and member of the European Parliament, the woman on the beast is now the official picture of the EU. He points out that the multimillion-dollar new parliament building located in Brussels, Belgium, contains a dome with a colossal painting, three times life-size, of a woman riding a beast.

In Strasbourg, France, the rival parliamentary building (the one with the Tower of Babel) features a mural of a naked woman riding a beast. Likewise, the new Brussels headquarters of the

---

[65] Dr. David Reagan, "Europe in Bible Prophecy Introduction," article taken from https://lamblion.com/xfiles/publications/magazines/Lamplighter_MayJun01_EuropeanUnion.pdf

Council of Europe contains a bronze statue of a woman riding a beast, and the beast is depicted riding on waves, just as is described in Revelation 17.

THE GATE OF BABYLON REBUILT[66]

The gate of Babylon was to be rebuilt by Saddam Hussein. But before he could complete it, the original Babylon came to Germany. Historically, the Persians inherited the spirit of Babylon when they captured the city in 539 BC. Alexander had ten thousand men rebuild the temple of Marduk, and they offered daily sacrifices to the dragon god until Alexander's premature death in 323 BC.

By the year 64 BC, Rome had overthrown the Greeks to become the New World Empire. Daniel prophesied that this empire would continue in various forms until the return of Christ. Through the Romans, the spirit of Babylon came against the people of God; the temple was destroyed in AD 70, and the Jews were scattered throughout the world in exile until the miraculous reestablishment of Israel in 1948.

After the collapse of Imperial Rome, the popes of Rome designated excessive European kings as Holy Roman Emperors, and as political leaders of the people of the Holy Roman Empire. The title of the Holy Roman Emperor was held by the Germanic Hapsburg

---

[66] An excellent documentary on this subject, *The Rape of Europe,* was produced by Rev. David Hathaway. More information can be found at http://www.propheticvision.org.uk. This matter of this part of the book was transcribed from the video, *The Rape of Europe* © 2004.

Dynasty[67] for hundreds of years. They also held the title king of Jerusalem, granted in perpetuity after the European crusaders took on the Turks in 1061. In 1898, Germany's Wilhelm II visited the Holy Land as the king of Jerusalem. A year later, he began excavations in the ancient site of Jerusalem. In 1913, he brought to Berlin the first pieces of the gate. The processional way was covered with 337 snake dragons, which were Babylon's entrance to hell on earth.

A year later, in 1914, Germany warred with the world. Ten million people died in the next four years. By 1930, the entire processional way of Babylon was erected in Berlin. It is possible that Hitler was possessed by Satan himself as he murdered six million Jews during the Holocaust in Europe. Hitler's Second World War, from 1939–1945, was truly hell on earth. More than fifty-five million people died worldwide.

Berlin was divided between the superpowers of the east and west. While East Berlin retained the Istar Gate of Babylon, West Germany moved into a period of grace. Chancellor Adenauer, a devout Christian and a lifetime opponent of Nazism, recognized the biblical truth that God would bless those who blessed the Jews.[68]

At a time when his own country was lying in ruins, he offered to help to rebuild Israel. When the German postwar economic miracle began, this change reunited East and West Germany in 1990. Today, Germany's economy is still in crisis.

---

67 http://galileo.rice.edu/gal/urban/html, http://www.answers.com/topic/holy-roman-emper- or-2.

68 http://en.wikipedia.org/wiki/CD.

The father of King Nebuchadnezzar laid the foundation stone for the first Babylon. There is a note that was written at that time, "At the best of the gods Nabu and Marduk, who ordered me to secure the foundations of Babylon on the very heart of the underworld so that its head can vibe with heaven itself, I have bowed my neck and done as I have been commanded." Berlin, with the gates of Babylon, is now once again the capital city of a united Germany.

During the Second World War, Hitler outlined the new European policy for the control of postwar Europe under the following headings, "The Common European Currency," "The Harmonization of European Rates of Exchange," "The European Community," "The European Agriculture Order," and so on.

Despite his defeat, identical plans to Hitler's are being implemented in the European Union today. Whose plans are they? Christian believers are warned in Revelation 18:4–5: "Come out of her, my people, so that you will not share in her sins, so that you will not receive any of her plagues; for her sins are piled up to heaven, and God has remembered her crimes."

The Bible warns us in Daniel 2:33–34 and Revelation 19:11 that the spirit of Babylon will continue its activities. The treaty of the Roman Empire has brought about a gathering of nations in the European Union.

Sadly, Europe has a concentration of satanic activity, just like any other region in the world. The concentration has intensified because Europe plays an important role in the end-time fulfillment of biblical prophecy.

SATAN'S SEAT REBUILT

REVELATION 2:13a KJV

I know thy works, and where thou dwellest, even where Satan's seat is.

Only one place in the entire Bible is described as the seat of Satan. In modern times, this seat has been reassembled in Berlin, Germany. The gigantic altar of Pergamum dominates the Museum of Pergamum in Berlin. Originally from Asia Minor—modern Turkey today—the temple of Pergamum was the center of emperor worship. The price of refusing to worship the emperor as god was ritual murder at the altar. Early Christians were martyred for their faith in Christ on this altar.

German archaeologist Karl Humann found the altar to be in perfect condition in early 1800. He then carefully shipped every stone to Berlin. In 1902, Kaiser Wilhelm II celebrated its erection in Berlin as the proudest moment of his life with an extravagant festival dedicated to the pagan gods.

It is significant to note that, within a short time, the history of Germany was dominated by a sequence of events that could only be attributed to satanic control. While the rest of the world, like London, Wales, and America, were receiving the outpouring of the Holy Spirit in 1904, the German churches rejected the move of the Holy Spirit, regarding the move and its manifestations as the work of the devil.

As a result of this declaration from the German churches, they became the modern seat of biblical criticism, with liberal theology questioning the truth of the Bible and undermining the very foundations of faith. And this diabolical lie spread worldwide. The allegation that the Bible is not the inspired Word of God was promoted; instead, the lie was propagated that it is only a historical storybook, a collection of poetry and myths (especially with regard to the incarnation of Christ).

With the long European church tradition steeped in anti-Semitism, all of this paved the way for Hitler's Holocaust of the Jews, with almost no protest from the leadership of the church. Hitler was so impressed with the altar of Pergamum of Berlin in 1934 that he commissioned a grand reproduction to be made for his Nazi rallies. From the very seat of Satan, he decreed death to the Jews and all those not possessing Aryan blood.

Mainstream churches officially supported Hitler at that time. Many Germans from all denominations paid with their lives for holding fast their faith in Christ and for sheltering Jews during the Nazi persecution. After many years now, the churches in Germany are united and are fervently praying for revival.

The headquarters of Hitler, which were destroyed during the war, have now been completely rebuilt. After fifty years, the government of Germany moved into this same building in Berlin, where the seat of Satan is located.

A BALANCED VIEW OF SPIRITUAL WARFARE

I believe the Body of Christ needs to maintain a balanced view about spiritual warfare. During the last twenty years, there has been an unhealthy level of overemphasis on the role of spiritual warfare in the life of the Church. Believers are more conscious of demons around them than the ever-abiding presence of God.

Many have become unnecessary casualties of spiritual warfare as they entered into certain realms of the spiritual world without the calling, the anointing, and the specific leading of the Lord. Some stepped into these realms "by mistake" due to being overzealous after attending some spiritual warfare school or seminar. Some stepped into these satanic grounds by operating under a false anointing[69] not given or authorized by the Lord. The sons of Sceva in Acts 19:13–16 operated in such a deceptive authority that even the demons did not recognize them.

Many prayer and deliverance ministries have "unnecessarily" taught deeper teachings on spiritual warfare, either to bring in revenue for their ministries or to produce more spiritual warriors.

The servants of God who are spiritually mature and have walked for many years with the Lord can handle any onslaught of the enemy. But when they teach deeper teachings of spiritual warfare to young believers whose spirits are not mature enough, it leads to those young believers becoming needless casualties of spiritual warfare.

---

69 Steven Francis, *Fragrance Plus Anointing* (Rivers of Life Visions International, 2003).

Some just stand on one Scripture: "I have given you authority to trample on snakes and scorpions and to overcome all the power of the enemy; nothing will harm you" (Luke 10:19), and they operate unwisely in matters of spiritual warfare.

It is like saying that since a baby is surrounded by water inside the mother's womb, every person will know how to swim after they are born. And as a result, they encourage everyone to jump into the ocean. As crazy as it sounds, this analogy applies to leading younger believers into deeper dimensions of the spiritual world without the necessary, sufficient spiritual wisdom.

Look at what Jesus said to His disciples: "The knowledge of the secrets of the kingdom of God has been given to you, but to others I speak in parables" (Luke 8:10).

JOHN 16:12 AMPC

I have still many things to say to you, but you are not able to bear them or to take them upon you or to grasp them now.

Our Lord Jesus taught His disciples in measures according to their spiritual capacity to receive. In John 16:13, He assured them that when the Holy Spirit came, He would guide them and teach them the truth. Even now, the Lord trains His disciples in the same manner, always giving the revelation of the Word according to a person's level of spiritual maturity. Each revelation is based on a person's growth, anointing level, and call.

What I am sharing with you is not intended to belittle anyone or lift up my or others' spiritual importance. Too many times,

I have met believers who are more interested to find out which demon is controlling their city than knowing what God has planned for their lives.

No ministry on earth can send Satan back to hell. No ministry on earth can release the glory of God as they wish. We can all pray for God's glory to come based on our repentance and prayer (2 Chronicles 7:14), but we cannot command the glory that belongs to God. Do not become too carried away by ministry advertisements and catchy slogans in colorful brochures.

Jesus is coming back for a triumphant church. We are a part of His mighty army, which God is raising up in these end times.

OPS BRIEFING 6

THE RISING ARMIES OF THE LORD

Throughout the Bible, we can always see the thread of divine warfare between good and evil. The war that started in the heavenlies will soon come to an end. The Body of Christ is going to play a great role in this war, which Christ has already won.

The armies of God are of divine origin. They obey the divine laws of the Kingdom of God. They obey a Commander whom they have not seen, and they fight an invisible enemy.

2 CORINTHIANS 10:4 AMPC

For the weapons of our warfare are not physical [weapons of flesh and blood], but they are mighty before God for the overthrow and destruction of strongholds.

EPHESIANS 6:12 AMPC

For we are not wrestling with flesh and blood [contending only with physical opponents], but against the despotisms, against the powers, against [the master spirits who are] the world rulers of this present darkness, against the spirit forces of wickedness in the heavenly (supernatural) sphere.

The weapons we use in the Spirit are not weapons of mass destruction; instead, ours are the weapons of righteousness and of the Spirit (Ephesians 6:13–18). The armies of the world pride themselves in their own strength, and they compete with one another, but the armies of the Lord are to live their lives as living sacrifices (Romans 12:1; 8:29; Philippians 2:5). The motto of this divine army is this: "He must increase, but I must decrease" (John 3:30 NKJV).

2 CORINTHIANS 6:3–10

We put no stumbling block in anyone's path, so that our ministry will not be discredited. Rather, as servants of God we commend ourselves in every way: in great endurance; in troubles, hardships and distresses; in beatings, imprisonments and riots; in hard work, sleepless nights and hunger; in purity, understanding, patience and kindness; in the Holy Spirit and in sincere love; in truthful speech and in the power of God; with weapons of righteousness in the right hand and in the left; through glory and dishonor, bad report and good report; genuine, yet regarded as impostors; known, yet regarded as unknown; dying, and yet we live on; beaten, and yet not killed; sorrowful, yet always rejoicing; poor, yet making many rich; having nothing, and yet possessing everything.

This army of Christ will have divine protection (Exodus 23:20–22; Daniel 10:13; Revelation 12:7) all around them as they obey the divine principles of spiritual warfare. The Lord Himself fights for them (Deuteronomy 20:4; 1 Samuel 17:47). This army walks not in the pride of the flesh. Rather, they march, singing songs of deliverance: "Not by might nor by power, but by My spirit, says the LORD" (Zechariah 4:6 NKJV), for "we are more than conquerors through Him who loved us" (Romans 8:37 NKJV). The Lord Himself becomes their shield of victory (Psalm 18:35), and He always causes them to triumph in Him (2 Corinthians 2:14).

Soldier of Christ, this same overcoming power has been given to you (Luke 10:19). You are to walk in His strength, declaring, "Greater is He that is in you, than he that is in the world" (1 John 4:4 KJV).

The Lord Jesus has promised that the gates of hell will not prevail against the Church (Matthew 16:18) and that no wickedness can overcome you when you walk in Him and obey His will (Jeremiah 1:19; 15:20). In the book of Revelation, we are called to be nothing less than overcomers (1 John 5:4–5; Revelation 2:7, 11, 17, 26; 3:5, 12, 27; 21:7).

Let us study some armies of the Bible and prophetically learn what it takes to be a part of the Lord's army. The Lord showed me the different armies that will bear different characteristics of the anointings carried by the prophets. Though all anointings are from the Holy Spirit, the Lord graciously shares them with the names of the prophets for identity purposes.

During one of my twenty-one days of fasting, after prayer, I went to take a shower. The moment I entered the bathroom, I was transported in the Spirit to a place in heaven where all the prophets of the Bible were lined up. I could see a big group. Then the Lord Jesus spoke to me in an audible voice, "All these prophets died in controversies. They prophesied events beyond their lifetime. I showed them what I was about to do hundreds of years ahead of time. But I say to you, before I come back again, all their prophecies will come to pass." Upon hearing this, my eyes were full of tears at the mercies of the Lord. I was translated back to the bathroom.

JOEL'S ARMY

During December 2001, I was waiting upon the Lord with fasting and prayer for His Word for the following year. The Word of the Lord came to me about the end-time army that was going to rise up on the face of the earth. This prophecy was published in our ministry magazine.[70]

1. God is going to increase His battalion upon the face of the earth.

JOEL 2:11

The Lord thunders at the head of his army; his forces are beyond number, and mighty are those who obey his

[70] Steven Francis, *Harvest Glory* (Singapore: Rivers of Life Visions International, 2002, Vol. 8, Issue 1).

> *command. The day of the* L*ORD is great; it is dreadful. Who can endure it?*

The people of God are going to be raised up by the mighty arm of the Lord. The grace of God will be poured upon the ones who are hungry for Jesus, and He will raise them up to be mighty in Christ. Even the least among us will be a match for a hundred (1 Chronicles 12:14). Amen! God will raise this army up out of the stones, out of the ordinary men and women who trust in Him (Matthew 3:9). Let us be the army that fights for the right cause!

No single minister, ministry, church, Bible college, institute, or country can claim exclusiveness to this army. They will come from everywhere, across the nations, from all denominational platforms. The Church has divided itself according to her theological persuasions, but God does not. He knows how to spark a fire through His Word, cause a reformation, and stir the fires of revival so that men and women will be released for this supernatural call and work.

The Bible says that *"forces are beyond* ("great" KJV) *number and mighty are those who obey his command."* What a delight it will be for Jesus when His army obeys His every command. The Hebrew word for *great* is *rab*, meaning "abundant in quantity, size, rank, quality, exceeding, full, great, master, more, much, plenteous, and process of time."

The Body of Christ is going to grow by leaps and bounds. She is going to rise in great numbers throughout the world. No government in the world can stop the fire of the Holy Spirit from spreading. No devil can stop souls from getting saved. The quality of the disciples will greatly reflect the work of the Holy Spirit in them. Through the process of time, these disciples will be sent out into the harvest field.

There will be more miraculous salvations than ever recorded in history. The strength and the creativity of the Holy Spirit will undergird the evangelistic efforts of the churches and parachurch ministries, and it will yield a hundredfold harvest for the Kingdom of God.

The ministries that walk in the will of the Father will be filled with the might of the Holy Spirit (Ephesians 3:16) to be a powerful force on the earth. Inner strength will enable the Body of Christ to sail the mighty waters of faith and trials and finish the race set by God (Matthew 12:11). Each of these churches and ministries will become masters in what they do for Him through the wisdom and understanding of the Holy Spirit.

One example of such a ministry is that of Reverend Reinhard Bonnke. In one of his books, he wrote, "Once our ministry sailed from prophecy to prophecy, today, it rides from fulfillment to fulfillment. For more than twenty years, I carried a divine promise in my heart that one day we should see a million souls converted in a single meeting. In Lagos, Nigeria, on Sunday the 12th of November 2000, this came to pass when our co-workers recorded 1,093,745 decisions for Christ. We have acquired sound systems to reach crowds bigger than perhaps ever addressed before on earth by one man face to face. Arrogant presumption? If the Crucified One is to 'see the labor of His soul, and be satisfied' (Isa. 53:11), dare we think in smaller terms?"[71] To date (2016), seventy-five million people have been saved through his ministry.

The fresh fire of the Holy Spirit must descend upon the Church once again to make us firebrands for Christ. The Church in the book of Acts was a community on fire for God, a people of faith, a hothouse of fearless evangelists made up of all the eight things listed below:[72]

- They were separated people (Acts 2:41).
- They were steadfast people (Acts 2:42, 46–47).
- They were sanctified people in holy fear (Acts 2:43a).
- They were spectacular people (Acts 2:43b).
- They were singular people (Acts 2:44).
- They were sacrificial people (Acts 2:45).
- They were successful people (Acts 2:47).
- They were suffering people (Acts 5:41).

2. Blow the Trumpet and Sound the Alarm

JOEL 2:1

Blow the trumpet in Zion; sound the alarm on my holy hill. Let all who live in the land tremble, for the day of the Lord *is coming. It is close at hand.*

---

[71] Reinhard Bonnke, *Evangelism by Fire* (Full Flame GmbH, 2001), xii.

[72] As quoted in *Day of His Power 40 Days Devotional* (Singapore, LoveSingapore, 2005), dated July 10.

The angel of the Lord has blown the trumpet to raise the army of the Lord. Heaven is getting ready for the biggest showdown with the enemy and for the Second Coming of Christ Jesus, our Lord. On December 30, 2004, while I was fasting and praying, I heard the voice of the Lord saying, "The trumpet has sounded, and a little more time is given for the people to return to the Lord."

At the sound of the alarm, the resurrected power of Jesus (John 11:25) will raise the weak, the poor, the foolish of the world, and the people looked down upon (1 Corinthians 1:27) to be His army, like the description in Ezekiel 37. This army will be built by the hand of Jesus through the deepening and heavy dealings of the Holy Spirit (Ezekiel 37:7–8).

The Lord will raise up the Lazarus company whom He has been pruning for years with love, those who will hear the Master's call and respond to this hour. These men and women will come out of their tombs of weakness and will receive a fresh anointing from the Father God. They will flow in a heavy anointing of healing that will result in salvation of souls. This army will have a single-minded devotion to Jesus in utter simplicity. The Lord will handpick this army, like how Gideon's army was handpicked, to defeat the works of the devil and to declare the Lordship of Christ among the nations (Judges 7:1–7).

The late Reverend David Wilkerson prophesied, "God is at work doing something hidden and quiet—and it is so supernatural, it's beyond human comprehension. Yet what He is doing right now is going to affect the whole world in these last days. God is preparing a small but powerful army of Christians! This army is going to be the most dedicated on the face of the earth. And the Lord will come forth to command them to do exploits and shake hell. He is going to close out the ages with a pure, devoted, fearless remnant!

"When I speak of a holy remnant in training, I do not mean an army of preachers, evangelists, and missionaries. I am talking about ordinary saints—lovers of Jesus who themselves will be signs and wonders to the world, full of peace and calm. God doesn't want a professional army trained in man's methods. He wants men and women who are trained in prayer by the Holy Spirit! He is seeking believers who are shut in with Him, preparing their hearts before Him, learning to hear His voice. I urge you to get alone with God and let Him begin to speak to you. Ask Him to reveal the sin in your life. Forsake all that the Holy Spirit convicts you of. And make yourself available to Him by giving yourself to prayer. Then you will be a ready soldier in His great, last-day remnant army."[73]

3. The Supernatural Favor of God on Them

JOEL 2:3 NKJV

A fire devours before them, and behind them a flame burns; the land is like the Garden of Eden before them, and behind them a desolate wilderness; surely nothing shall escape them.

This army will walk in the favor of God in all its endeavors for the Kingdom of God. Just as God supported Moses with supernatural

---

[73] http://www.tscpulpitseries.org/english/1990s/ts940613.html.

manifestations, this army, too, will be backed up with the awesome power of God and angelic protection (Exodus 14:19–20).

The Lord gave a promise to Joshua: "Every place that the sole of your foot will tread upon I have given you, as I said to Moses" (Joshua 1:3 NKJV). This is the same kind of promise of possession the Lord is giving to the end-time Church (Joshua 1:5; Mark 16:20). This army will have a double-portion anointing to establish the Kingdom of God in every nation.

As this end-time army obeys the command of the Lord to bear witness of the crucified Christ, He will confirm His words with His power. The problem is that many churches and ministries are busy convincing the world of their ministry names. They have become too busy propagating their philosophies instead of being busy fulfilling the Great Commission.

4. THEY RUN WITH SPEED LIKE HORSES

JOEL 2:4–5 NKJV

Their appearance is like the appearance of horses; and like swift steeds, so they run. With a noise like chariots over mountaintops they leap, like the noise of a flaming fire that devours the stubble, like a strong people set in battle array.

Horses in the Bible are symbols of power (Psalm 20:7), of strength (Job 39:19), and of conquest (Revelation 19:19). Horses are also important symbols of being ready for battle (Jeremiah 46:4; Zechariah 10:3; Revelation 9:7, 9; 19:14, 19).

Horses were used in warfare as early as the nineteenth century BC. In fact, much training was required to overcome the horse's natural aversion to the smell of blood and its natural disinclination to trample down a person. A warhorse's training would generally address its responsiveness to being controlled without reins, its tolerance for the noises of battle, and its adaptability to weapons and the armor the rider would be using. In addition, some warhorses were trained to kick, strike, and even bite on command, thus becoming weapons in the extended arsenal of the warriors they carried.[74] The quarter horse can run up to a speed of 76.44 kilometers per hour (47.50 mph).[75]

Sitting on a horse gives the rider a majestic and glorious look, and this is the appearance of the end-time army. They will have a majestic look about them. I believe this speaks of their spirit of devotion for the cause of their Master.

Our Lord Jesus, while He was alive on this earth, rode on a donkey, but when He comes back to the earth, He will ride on a white horse with a glorious retinue of tens of thousands of His saints and angels. Oh! What a sight to behold!

REVELATION 19:11–14 NKJV

Now I saw heaven opened, and behold, a white horse. And He who sat on him was called Faithful and True, and in righteousness He judges and makes war. His eyes were like a flame of fire, and on His head were many crowns. He had

74 http://en.wikipedia.org/wiki/War_horse.

75 http://www.factmonster.com/ipka/A0004737.html.

> *a name written that no one knew except Himself. He was clothed with a robe dipped in blood, and His name is called The Word of God. And the armies in heaven, clothed in fine linen, white and clean, followed Him on white horses.*

Once, I was admitted to the hospital due to food poisoning during a mission trip to India. My blood pressure dropped so low that I had to be hospitalized for six days. I was put on drips, and my body was dehydrated. My spirit was down, and I felt lousy. I thought to myself, "Maybe I just need to slow down on the mission trips and so on."

My brother came to visit me in the hospital. As he was about to leave, he closed his eyes to pray. The anointing of the Holy Spirit came on him, and the Lord gave him a word from Jeremiah 12:5: "If you have raced with men on foot and they have worn you out, how can you compete with horses?"

I thought to myself, "What a prayer to receive while I am sick to my stomach in the hospital!" But the Lord was lifting me up from a pity-party state of mind with the arms of a strong father, and He was putting me back on my feet. It was like He was saying, "I have a long way for you to go and more places for you to minister. I am going to increase the speed of My directives for you to do My work."

This army will have the ability to run fast to fulfill the bidding of the Lord. They will move in divine timing (Romans 13:11; Ephesians 5:16). The Holy Spirit will become the bridle on these horses to run the race of the Lord (James 3:3).

These men and women will have a deeper sense of the divine urgency in their hearts to complete their God-given tasks within a certain time frame (Isaiah 5:19, 26). And this army will obey precise timing. These men and women are not going to display sad, sorry faces for signing up for this army; instead, their faces will have the appearance of horses ready for battle, the faces of trained warriors.

5. An Obedient and Persistent Army

JOEL 2:7–8 NKJV

They run like mighty men, they climb the wall like men of war; every one marches in formation, and they do not break ranks. They do not push one another; every one marches in his own column. Though they lunge between the weapons, they are not cut down.

What a strength and a display of unity! This army knows their limits and their ranks. They know their part in the work of the Lord. When they are sent to do a job, they will complete it while the other folks in the church are playing games to see who will win and who is the greatest and the loudest.

This army will follow orders. They know their mission and battle plans, and they will not engage in battles that are not theirs. They do not break ranks or run around doing their own thing. They do not push one another to provoke, challenge, or intimidate. Instead, everyone marches in his or her own column.

2 TIMOTHY 2:3–4 AMPC

Take [with me] your share of the hardships and suffering [which you are called to endure] as a good (first-class) soldier of Christ Jesus. No soldier when in service gets entangled in the enterprises of [civilian] life; his aim is to satisfy and please the one who enlisted him.

This is a picture of the end-time Church that is very determined to live her life for Jesus. She has only one purpose, and that is to fight the battles of the Lord!

6. The Army of the Lord Is Going to Receive New Strategies About Learning to Use the Weapons of Warfare.

There are many lessons for this army to learn, and the Holy Spirit will give them the necessary wisdom and revelation. New revelations of strategic prayer warfare will be revealed. God will use His servants around the world to release these strategies for every tribe and every nation. We cannot afford to assume that a method that works in one place can be duplicated for use in another nation.

7. The Lord Is Going to Bring Satan and His Works in Circles and Defeat His Very Schemes.

In 2 Chronicles 20:1, we read about "the Moabites, the Ammonites, and with them the Meunites came against Jehoshaphat to battle." Although Jehoshaphat feared the news, just like any one of us would do, he "set himself [determinedly, as his vital need] to seek the Lord; he proclaimed a fast in all Judah" (v. 3 AMPC).

And the Lord, upon seeing the heart of Jehoshaphat and his dependence on Him, spoke through Jahaziel: "Be not afraid or dismayed at this great multitude; for the battle is not yours, but God's" (v. 15 AMPC). However, the Lord said that although they did not need to fight the battle, the army still needed to take its position on the battlefield and see the deliverance of the Lord.

The king "appointed singers to sing to the Lord and praise Him in their holy [priestly] garments as they went out before the army, saying, 'Give thanks to the Lord, for His mercy and loving-kindness endure forever!'" (v. 21 AMPC). The Lord set an ambush for the enemies, and they slaughtered one another. The Bible says that "the Lord had made them to rejoice over their enemies" (v. 27 AMPC).

Likewise, the Lord will do the same for His army. The Lord will thwart the plans of the enemy. The wisdom of God will prevail against the cunning devices of the enemy! We will win!

DAVID'S MIGHTY MEN OF VALOR

The story of David's most valiant warriors unfolds in 2 Samuel 23:8–23. It is important to study the character, the dedication, and the spirit of these men. We can draw parallels from which the end-time army of the Lord can glean.

The word *mighty* from 2 Samuel 23:8 comes from the Hebrew word *gibbor*, from which we get the words *powerful, champion, warrior, excellence, valiant,* and *strong.*

How can the soldiers of the Lord become mighty in Him?

1. The Ability of the Holy Spirit

First, to become powerful, you must have the power and the ability of the Holy Spirit working in your life (Acts 1:8). You must learn to walk in the authority of God in your life.

LUKE 10:19 AMPC

Behold! I have given you authority and power to trample upon serpents and scorpions, and [physical and mental strength and ability] over all the power that the enemy [possesses]; and nothing shall in any way harm you.

2. Men of Courage and Boldness

Second, to become a champion, you must become a person of courage and boldness.

ACTS 4:13

When they saw the courage of Peter and John and realized that they were unschooled, ordinary men, they were astonished and they took note that these men had been with Jesus.

ACTS 4:29

Now, Lord, consider their threats and enable your servants to speak your word with great boldness.

1 CORINTHIANS 16:13

Be on your guard; stand firm in the faith; be men of courage; be strong.

3. Men of Substance, a Trained Force

Third, to become a warrior, you must train yourself in the Spirit and be godly (1 Timothy 4:7). When you combine the Hebrew words *gibbor* ("mighty") and *chayil* ("men of valor"), you get the phrase *"a proven warrior."*

You must prove yourself to be worthy of the calling of God upon your life (Philippians 1:27; 1 Thessalonians 2:12). Many want respect without paying the price. They desire positions of honor and authority without going through the ranks of servanthood.

1 TIMOTHY 1:4 AMPC

Nor to give importance to or occupy themselves with legends (fables, myths) and endless genealogies, which foster and promote useless speculations and questionings rather than acceptance in faith of God's administration and the divine training that is in faith (in that leaning of the entire human personality on God in absolute trust and confidence).

1 TIMOTHY 6:11 AMPC

But as for you, O man of God, flee from all these things; aim at and pursue righteousness (right standing with God and true goodness), godliness (which is the loving fear of God and being Christlike), faith, love, steadfastness (patience), and gentleness of heart.

Spend your time wisely by using the available time to train yourself in what God has called you to do. There are many who want to come into the full-time ministry with a wrong mentality—thinking it is the easiest or least-demanding job, that it is glamorous, or that it gives them more time for the family at home. This is obviously wrong.

Train yourself in the Spirit through prayer and the study of the Word of God. Pursue the righteousness of God for your life and ministry.

4. Men Who Excel

Fourth, to excel in the Lord's work, you need to balance the power of the Lord in your life with the character of Jesus. Earnestly desire to excel in the gifts that build the Church. Some desire the power gifts to stand out from others, but such desires are driven by wrong motives. Every gift from the Lord should build up the Church.

1 CORINTHIANS 14:12 AMPC

So it is with yourselves; since you are so eager and ambitious to possess spiritual endowments and manifestations of the [Holy] Spirit, [concentrate on] striving to excel and to abound [in them] in ways that will build up the church.

5. Valiant men

Fifth, to become valiant, you must fight the good fight of faith (1 Timothy 6:12). You must possess a level of strength and the power of His might in your inner man (Ephesians 6:10). The authority of God must be seen in your prayer and preaching. People must witness the presence of the Lord in your ministry (Matthew 7:29; Mark 3:14–15).

6. Men of strength

Lastly, to become a person filled with divine strength, you must learn to flow in the supernatural realm of God. Be strong from the inside out. You will learn to walk and talk in the Spirit rather than by the wisdom of the flesh.

EPHESIANS 3:16 AMPC

May He grant you out of the rich treasury of His glory to be strengthened and reinforced with mighty power in the inner man by the [Holy] Spirit [Himself indwelling your innermost being and personality].

1 CORINTHIANS 2:4–5 AMPC

And my language and my message were not set forth in persuasive (enticing and plausible) words of wisdom, but they were in demonstration of the [Holy] Spirit and power [a proof by the Spirit and power of God, operating on me and stirring in the minds of my hearers the most holy emotions and thus persuading them], so that your faith might not rest in the wisdom of men (human philosophy), but in the power of God.

The mighty men of David were mighty because of their courage and their natural fighting skills. But we who are of the Spirit must possess the qualities of a spiritual warrior to be in the Lord's army.

I admire the dedication these mighty men had toward David. When David's men heard that he was thirsty and desired to drink water from the well near the gate of Bethlehem, they broke through enemy lines, drew water from the desired well, and carried it back to David (2 Samuel 23:15–17). Such was their love for their commander and king!

What did David do when he realized that his men had risked their lives to fulfill his desire? David refused to drink the water, and he poured it out before the Lord. He said, "Is it not the blood of men who went at the risk of their lives?"

To a dedicated team, God gives a dedicated leader. To serve in the Kingdom of God, we need unity at all levels of leadership. We need a healthy team that brings glory to the name of the Lord Jesus Christ. Serving the Lord requires that we take many risks.

NOT FOR THE GLORY

2 SAMUEL 23:18–23

Abishai the brother of Joab son of Zeruiah was chief of the Three. He raised his spear against three hundred men, whom he killed, and so he became as famous as the Three.

Was he not held in greater honor than the Three? He became their commander, even though he was not included among them. Benaiah son of Jehoiada was a valiant fighter from Kabzeel, who performed great exploits. He struck down two of Moab's best men. He also went down into a pit on a snowy day and killed a lion. And he struck down a huge Egyptian. Although the Egyptian had a spear in his hand, Benaiah went against him with a club. He snatched the spear from the Egyptian's hand and killed him with his own spear. Such were the exploits of Benaiah son of Jehoiada; he too was as famous as the three mighty men. He was held in greater honor than any of the Thirty, but he was not included among the Three. And David put him in charge of his bodyguard.

Did you notice something out of the ordinary in this passage? Both of the men—Abishai, who speared three hundred men, and Benaiah, who was a valiant fighter—were famous commanders and were held in greater honor than the rest of the team. Yet they were not included among the top three. And it did not bother them!

Beloved of the Lord, are we missing something in the Body of Christ? What we are witnessing today is the exact opposite of what has always been the culture of heaven, which is to serve and honor others!

MATTHEW 23:11–12 AMPC

He who is greatest among you shall be your servant. Whoever exalts himself [with haughtiness and empty pride] shall be humbled (brought low), and whoever humbles himself [whoever has a modest opinion of himself and behaves accordingly] shall be raised to honor.

We are the Body of Christ. We are called to stand side by side with each other, and present ourselves before our Master. Each of us has been called to obey specific directives from the Lord. Another's call may not make sense to you. Each person's calling will only make sense to the one who has received that call. Do not judge by the denomination that he is from or what color his skin is, but rather judge him by the fruit he bears for the Kingdom of God (Matthew 7:16–20; John 7:24).

This was the heart cry of Jesus: "'If I do not do the works of My Father, do not believe Me; but if I do, though you do not believe Me, believe the works, that you may know and believe that the Father is in Me, and I in Him.' Therefore they sought again to seize Him, but He escaped out of their hand" (John 10:37–39 NKJV).

EZEKIEL'S ARMY

The anointing of Ezekiel's army carries a strong mandate to reach out to souls. Their ministry will be marked with an anointing of supernatural power accompanied by signs and wonders. I want to share briefly on this from Ezekiel 37.

EZEKIEL 37:1–2

The hand of the LORD was upon me, and he brought me out by the Spirit of the LORD and set me in the middle of a valley; it was full of bones. He led me back and forth among them, and I saw a great many bones on the floor of the valley, bones that were very dry.

1. A Defining Moment, A Spiritual Experience

The phrase *"brought me up"* in Ezekiel 37:1 comes from the Hebrew word *yatsa*, meaning "to come forth, to go out." The Hebrew language conveys the meaning that God uses what He has created to establish His purpose; an example of this is when He brought forth water from the rock (Deuteronomy 8:5). Another understanding of this meaning is "to be lifted up by a force," as in Ezekiel 8:3; 11:24.

In the New Testament, Philip was taken away by the Holy Spirit suddenly (Acts 8:39). The phrase *"took away"* comes from the Greek word *harpazo*. It is said to be an act of the Spirit of the Lord with regard to Philip, along with Paul being taken up to heaven in 2 Corinthians 12:2–4 and the rapture of the saints in 1 Thessalonians 4:17.

The point is not the place to which you are going to be taken, but rather, the point is the need to have definite spiritual experiences in your moments with God, where you wrestle with Him on your knees in prayer. That will become a defining moment in your life and ministry. This experience can come from the Word of God as revelation to your heart while you meditate on the Scriptures or as a spiritual encounter while waiting upon God in prayer. Without this, your ministry will be weak and without substance.

The Holy Spirit must pour Himself out upon the Body of Christ afresh once again. We need something bigger than the Azusa Street Revival. We need a power that will fill everyone, everywhere. No denomination can lay claim to any anointing that originates from heaven.

2. THE VALLEY OF SOULS

The Spirit of the Lord set Ezekiel in the middle of a valley full of dry bones. This speaks clearly of the valley of souls, where millions are perishing by the second. The prophet saw a valley, not a mountain.

Today, many want a million promises before they take the first step of faith in ministry. They want to see the gold, they want to see the money, and they want to see a big ministry. At times, my fellow soldier, God may want you to dig a trench and stay there until He orders you out of it. It is in the valley that you will see bones. And the Bible says the bones Ezekiel saw were very dry.

The Word of the Lord is this: Do not delay any longer your obedience to the voice of the Master. The bones are drying up in the valley, while believers are busy dressing themselves up with clothes of glamour.

Hudson Taylor, the missionary to China, said, "I almost wish I had a hundred bodies; they should be all devoted to my Savior in the missionary cause in China." Sadhu Sundar Singh said he wished that God would allow him to preach to the souls in hell as well as in heaven so that there would be no more souls left to be saved.

Your passion for souls will release the anointing of the Holy Spirit afresh upon you. What is the point of having a great name and a great ministry when you have lost your passion for souls?

Often, I am invited to speak to Bible college students. Many of these students are qualified in the natural to serve in any ministry. But the one thing I see lacking in their spirits is the passion for souls. Yes, once they complete their education, they will receive a beautiful graduation diploma, but the unction of the Holy Spirit will only come when there is a passion for souls in a person's heart.

3. The Prophetic Evangelism

EZEKIEL 37:4

Then he said to me, "Prophesy to these bones and say to them, 'Dry bones, hear the word of the Lord!"

There is going to be an increase of the prophetic leadings of the Lord, where the Holy Spirit will lead His sons and daughters supernaturally to witness to hearts that are ready to receive Christ. There will be miraculous conversions.

This was the experience of Philip when the Spirit of the Lord took him to minister to an Ethiopian eunuch, an important official in charge of all the treasury of Candace, queen of the Ethiopians, on the desert road that goes down from Jerusalem to Gaza in Acts 8:36.

Likewise, many hearts of political leaders will be softened and prepared to receive ministers of the Gospel, and their nations will hear the Gospel as the Lord wants to heal their lands.

4. Hear the Voice of the Lord

The word *hear* in Ezekiel 37:4 comes from the Hebrew word *shama*, meaning "an intense desire to obey or objective listening." We can also say it as "hearing with an intention to obey." The church that hears what the Holy Spirit is saying will bulldoze itself through the works of the enemy in these end times. Take time to hear the leading of the Lord. The anointing to overcome is given to the church that listens to the counsel of the Lord Jesus (Revelation 2:7, 17, 29; 3:6, 13, 22). Ezekiel heard the voice of the Lord and prophesied over the dry bones, and the power of God brought breath back into the bones, and they came to life (Ezekiel 37:10).

5. An Exceedingly Great Army

EZEKIEL 37:10 NKJV

So I prophesied as He commanded me, and breath came into them, and they lived, and stood upon their feet, an exceedingly great army.

Out of this supernatural resurrection comes an army that is exceedingly great. The word *exceeding* comes from the Hebrew word *meod*, meaning to be "diligent, loud, and quick." This word applies to the amount or quantity of a matter, as in Genesis 7:18,

"And the waters prevailed, and were increased greatly upon the earth" (KJV).

This word is also used in Psalm 47:9b: "For the shields of the earth belong to God; He is greatly exalted" (NKJV). The meaning here is that of "magnifying" and "exaltation." The same Hebrew word can also be translated as "might," as in Deuteronomy 6:5 (KJV), "And thou shalt love the Lord thy God with all thine heart, and with all thy soul, and with all thy might."

We can see the prophetic implication about this supernatural army, who will be raised up by the mighty power of God from ashes. This army will be exceeding in quantity. They will live for Jesus with all their hearts, souls, and might, and their sole purpose is to magnify and exalt the Lord on earth.

The word *great* in Ezekiel 37:10 comes from the Hebrew word *gadol*, meaning "great in number" (Genesis 12:2), "great in power" (Deuteronomy 4:37), and "great in value and importance" (Genesis 39:9). The word *gadol* also means "becoming great" and "growing up in wealth and prosperity."

GENESIS 26:12–13

Isaac planted crops in that land and the same year reaped a hundredfold, because the LORD blessed him. The man became rich, and his wealth continued to grow until he became very wealthy.

In these last days, the Ezekiel army will also be involved in businesses to bring wealth into the house of God. These will become Kingdom financiers and consultants. Through the blessings and the favor of God, they will accumulate wealth for end-time ministries. The anointing of Joseph and Daniel is part of this company. They will know how to conduct themselves with godliness and wisdom in the midst of the world and gather wealth for Kingdom purposes.

In the year 2017, I had a powerful encounter relating to Ezekiel's army. When in Singapore, my son Samuel John Francis experienced a heartbreak and was experiencing a difficult moment in his young life. We were standing outside the gate of the house near the veranda. As I was speaking to Samuel, I saw the similitude of Jesus behind him. The Lord then came from the back of Samuel and spoke to me, "Why are you so hard on your son? He belongs to the Ezekiel army. I will raise him up when his season comes. He is experiencing the hardness of life, and I am pruning him to the different stages of dryness. He will be raised up as My warrior in this end time." Upon hearing this, I realized that God was giving Samuel his testimony.

I was getting ready to preach in Egypt, the Open Heaven's Conference organized by Brother Sadhu Sundar Selvaraj. I was the speaker for the first session. I had many spiritual visitations and encounters with the Lord in heaven for this conference. I knew something new would take place.

Just before I left my hotel room for the session, I prayed for a few minutes. In front of me, in the spirit, a drawer opened up, and I saw many spiritual weapons. The Lord said, "Take whichever weapon you want." I saw a beautiful sword with the inscription,

"The sword of Elijah." I told the Lord, "I will take the sword of Elijah." When I took the sword, the sword entered my spirit.

When the session started, the Lord spoke to me, "Today, I will bring you to a place in hell where the souls are kept captive. You must do warfare. Continue to preach until I tell you when to pray."

The anointing was very strong on me as I taught the Word, but on another side of my mind, I was thinking what the Lord would tell me. While preaching, two lions entered the hallway. I did wonder, "Why are the lions here?" I continued preaching, and the Lord said, "Now, call the people to join you to pray for their unsaved loved ones, for their children." When I invited the people, hundreds ran forward and began to pray. The warfare anointing came upon us. I saw myself descending into the dark regions of hell. As we were descending, the lions who were with me used their sharp claws to tear through the darkness, and the light of God shone as we descended. As the light shone all around us, the demons were not able to stop us.

When I reached the bottom surface, I saw huge muscular demons strongly holding down a chain with iron balls to an anchor. I traced the chains with my eyes, wondering who they were holding onto. I saw the chains bound to the young people in bondage on earth through various addictions, lusts, and relationships. The demons knew that God would raise them up.

Then the lions who were with me used their claws to cut through the chains as they roared loudly. There was a sound of holiness. A holy boldness and strength entered my spirit. I could hear the people praying in the hall, roaring like a lion. At that moment, my spirit was back in my body, and we were praising God for His mercies on our children.

The next day during morning worship service, the anointing came upon us like a thick cloud. My son Samuel came forward to kneel and worship God, followed by many. It was the beginning of a breakthrough for many. Hallelujah!

Ezekiel's army will rise up out of the ashes of this world, and the Lord will raise them up with a powerful anointing to break the bondages of sin.

ZECHARIAH'S ARMY, THE STEALTH FORCE

ZECHARIAH 1:10

Then the man standing among the myrtle trees explained, "They are the ones the LORD has sent to go throughout the earth."

The army of Zechariah will play a major role in ushering in the Second Coming of our Lord Jesus Christ. The Lord will release His heavenly army to patrol the earth and to fulfill His decrees. The angels that are described in the book of Revelation for the opening of the seals, blowing the trumpets, and many other events belong to this company. Zechariah himself had a series of eight prophetic visions relating to the end times:

- The horseman among the myrtle trees (1:7–17).
- The four horns and the four craftsmen (1:18–21).
- A man with a measuring line (chapter 2).
- Clean garments for the high priest (chapter 3)
- The golden lampstand and the two olive trees (chapter 4)
- The flying scroll (5:1–4)
- The woman in a basket (5:5–11)
- The four chariots (6:1–8)

1. The Church and her ministers will be judged.

This army will declare the righteous judgments of the Lord to the Church and to her ministers. False ministers and ministries will fall away like stars from the heavens. They will become both a parable and a warning to others of the coming judgment that awaits those who take the name of the Lord in vain.

ZECHARIAH 10:3 AMPC

My anger is kindled against the shepherds [who are not true shepherds] and I will punish the goat leaders, for the Lord of hosts has visited His flock, the house of Judah, and will make them as His beautiful and majestic horse in the battle.

Those of us in the ministry are to be careful to watch over our own lives and walk in holiness before the Lord, lest we give Satan a right to accuse us before the presence of God (Zechariah 3). We must come out of the Babylonian ways and live as unto the Lord

(Zechariah 2:7). This is the season when the angel of the Lord is going forth to measure the Church (Zechariah 2:1).

2. The Church with the Might of God

ZECHARIAH 4:6 NKJV

So he answered and said to me: "This is the word of the LORD to Zerubbabel: 'Not by might nor by power, but by My Spirit,' says the LORD of hosts."

The Church will walk in the might of God in order to fulfill her work on this earth. As the oppressive spirit of the last days will make it harder for believers to live for Jesus, the Holy Spirit's anointing will cleanse them with the blood of Jesus and raise them up to be His witnesses.

No mountain can stand before the Church in the last days. The mountains of mounting problems and persecutions will become level ground in one sweep by the fire of the Holy Spirit (Zechariah 4:7). This move will be a window of opportunity for the Body of Christ to serve the Lord with all her heart one more time before the coming of Jesus.

The eyes of the Lord will be watching over His people and all the affairs of the nation (Zechariah 4:10). We are going to witness the ruling arm of Jesus, the King over the nations of the world. The Church has been harassed enough by extremists, terrorists, and militant religions. The supernatural protection of God will come upon her to fulfill the mandate of the Great Commission.

ZECHARIAH 2:5

"'And I myself will be a wall of fire around it,' declares the Lord, 'and I will be its glory within.'"

ZECHARIAH 2:8b NKJV

For he who touches you touches the apple of His eye.

The work that the Lord has started through His Bride, the Church, will be completed. The Lord will never leave His work undone. The Lord will raise up an army who will preach the holiness of God and bring the Refiner's Fire into the Church (Malachi 3:2).

ZECHARIAH 4:8–9

Then the word of the Lord came to me: "The hands of Zerubbabel have laid the foundation of this temple; his hands will also complete it. Then you will know that the Lord Almighty has sent me to you."

Regardless of how small your service to the Lord might be, do not despise it, but instead serve Him with all your heart in faithfulness (Zechariah 4:10). Neither harm nor danger can come against His Church when she walks right before the Lord. Satan can try his best, Jezebel can use her charm, and the wolves that spoil the vine can try their luck. But the Church of Jesus Christ has stood the test of time, and she will remain standing until the Second Coming of Jesus Christ. No gates of hell can prevail against the Lord's Church. No, not on the Lord's watch!

ZECHARIAH 9:8

But I will defend my house against marauding forces. Never again will an oppressor overrun my people, for now I am keeping watch.

3. Judgment on the Nations

The angels of the Lord will execute the Lord's judgments on the nations. The God of the Bible judges the wickedness of the nations. This is the season of fire of the Holy Spirit. Just look at the world news—what Jesus said would happen is happening now (Matthew 24).

ISAIAH 48:22

"There is no peace," says the Lord, *"for the wicked."*

There will be trouble for the wicked. The wicked are those who harbor evil in their hearts and do evil to others. This includes the believers who walk not in the light of the Scriptures but who continue to walk in their evil ways. There is no peace for them. God's judgment will come on those who mock the name of God, as well as those who attend church but prostitute themselves with the world.

Judgment will fall on the nations that are stained with the blood of the innocent and the helpless. These are the beginnings of birth pangs (Matthew 24:8), and secret plots and evil plans will be exposed (Luke 8:17).

ROMANS 1:18

The wrath of God is being revealed from heaven against all the godlessness and wickedness of men who suppress the truth by their wickedness.

Dr. John Stott wrote, "God's wrath is His holy hostility to evil, His refusal to condone it or come to terms with it, His judgment upon it."[76] There is a big difference between human anger and the righteous anger of the Lord. You can't think of God's anger from a human point of view. The anger of the Lord is controlled by His righteousness and justice.

The judgment of God is not only reserved until the end of all things, for some are already being judged now for their wickedness, as it has come up before the presence of God. How can anyone plead innocence in the courtroom of God? No one can escape the questioning of God.

4. The Fountain of God's Grace

ZECHARIAH 13:1

"On that day a fountain will be opened to the house of David and the inhabitants of Jerusalem, to cleanse them from sin and impurity."

[76] John Stott, *The Message of Romans: The Bible Speaks Today* (IVP, 1994), 72.

REVELATION 14:6–7

Then I saw another angel flying in midair, and he had the eternal gospel to proclaim to those who live on the earth—to every nation, tribe, language and people. He said in a loud voice, "Fear God and give him glory, because the hour of his judgment has come. Worship him who made the heavens, the earth, the sea and the springs of water."

Just before the return of Jesus, there is going to be a worldwide explosion of evangelism to reach the ends of the earth. I do believe that there will be a special "grace" of God made available to the Jews all over the world to accept Jesus as their personal Savior. Angels will be sent to proclaim the Gospel supernaturally to the Jews and to the nations.

MINISTRY TO THE JEWS

EZEKIEL 36:24

For I will take you out of the nations; I will gather you from all the countries and bring you back into your own land.

Angels will be sent out to cleanse people from sin and impurity. Many will come to Christ through terrible circumstances and wars during this season, which Zechariah prophesied. There will be cleansing from all forms of idolatry from the land (13:2), and false prophets will be removed, together with the spirit of impurity (13:3).

Once, I was called to pray for Israel in St. Louis, Missouri, in the United States. The Lord revealed wonderful visions of supernatural conversions that would take place among the Jews. I saw saints and angels being sent from heaven taking on human forms (i.e., mortality) to witness to high-ranking Jews and rabbis through signs and wonders. I saw angels being dispatched to protect the land of Israel from the enemy's plans and the secret invasion tactics of neighboring nations until the appointed time.

When I was back in Singapore, in another vision, I saw the Apostle Paul being knocked off of the horse, the incident that resulted in his conversion (Acts 9:3–16). In the same manner, the Lord said that many rabbis would receive supernatural encounters and be instantly converted to preach the coming of the King! Hallelujah!

THE NATION OF ISRAEL IS IMPORTANT

At the time of this writing (2006), a military fight has erupted between Israel and Lebanon. For some reason, the nation of Israel is always on the news. To the Christian world, this is of prime importance, as the nation of Israel plays a pivotal role in the fulfillment of the end-time prophecies of the Bible.

I wish to include an article that I read on the importance of Israel.[77] It was written by Marvin J. Rosenthal in his ministry's magazine, *Zion's Fire*.

---

[77] Marvin J. Rosenthal, *Zion's Fire* (Zion's Hope, Inc. Orlando, Florida, USA, Nov-Dec, 2004), Pg. 5

- Israel's importance on the world scene is not because of her national resources. The late Golda Meir, while prime minister of Israel, once quipped: "Moses wasn't too smart. He led our people to the one place in the Middle East where there is no oil." Israel does have chemicals, such as potash and bromide. These and other chemicals that are mined from the Dead Sea, as important as they are to Israel's economy, cannot compare to the natural resources of many other nations.
- Israel's importance is not because of her population. The nation of Israel is home to a meager 6,500,000 citizens, and only a little more than 5,500,000 are of Jewish descent. That number is less than a drop in the bucket when compared to most of the nations of the world.
- Israel's importance is certainly not because of her geographical size. Israel is a mere 8,019 square miles; by contrast, consider her Muslim neighbors:
  - Jordan is 35,637 square miles, more than four times the size of Israel.
  - Syria is 71,498 square miles, more than nine times the size of Israel.
  - Iraq is 168,754 square miles, more than twenty-one times the size of Israel.
  - Egypt is 386,662 square miles, more than forty-eight times the size of Israel.
  - Iran is 636,296 square miles, more than seventy-nine times the size of Israel.

- › Saudi Arabia is 756,984 miles, more than ninety-four times the size of Israel.

Also, consider some of the other major countries of the world:

- › China is 3,705,406 square miles, more than 462 times the size of Israel.
- › The United States is 3,717,812 square miles, more than 463 times the size of Israel.
- › The former Soviet Union is 6,592,771 square miles, more than 822 times the size of Israel.

- Israel's importance is not because of her military prowess. She possesses one of the best-trained, dedicated, and equipped armies in the world. But she is still vulnerable as a result of her small size.
- Some have suggested that Israel's importance is traced to the fact that through her people, Christ was born into the world.

An explanation for Israel's dramatic and disproportionate world importance is bound up in one overhanging reality: Israel is in conflict, not of her own choosing, but because it has been decreed by a sovereign God for the benefit of those who, through the ages, are destined to be heirs of God's grace.

5. THE SECOND COMING OF JESUS

ZECHARIAH 14:5b

Then the LORD my God will come, and all the holy ones with him.

Just before the Second Coming of Jesus, the nations of the world will gather to fight against Jerusalem. God will defend His chosen people.

ZECHARIAH 14:2, 3

I will gather all the nations to Jerusalem to fight against it; the city will be captured, the houses ransacked, and the women raped. Half of the city will go into exile, but the rest of the people will not be taken from the city.

Then the Lord will go out and fight against those nations, as he fights in the day of battle.

ZECHARIAH 14:12

This is the plague with which the Lord will strike all the nations that fought against Jerusalem: Their flesh will rot while they are still standing on their feet, their eyes will rot in their sockets, and their tongues will rot in their mouths.

During the war of the nations, millions will perish. Some prophecy teachers believe that Zechariah, through the Spirit of the Lord, described a nuclear explosion, which can generate 150 million degrees Fahrenheit in one millionth of a second. That is the only possible conclusion of how people's eyes and tongues can dissolve in their sockets and mouths before their bodies hit the ground.

Then, our Lord Jesus, the King of kings and the Lord of lords, will come with His saints and His angels. What a glorious sight it will be!

ZECHARIAH 14:9 NKJV

And the LORD shall be King over all the earth. In that day it shall be—"The LORD is one," And His name one.

So, who is the army of Zechariah's vision? Are they the left-behind saints? Are they those who will accept Jesus during the time of the Antichrist? Are they the remnant, the 144,000? My purpose is not to teach on the book of Revelation and end-time events but rather to give you a prophetic overview of the end-time events and our part to play in them.

I believe the vast armies of heavenly angels will do the bidding of the Lord of Hosts. This war will be both a physical and a supernatural war. The superpowers of this world cannot stop this supernatural army.

Someone once asked, "Since prior to the Second Coming of Jesus, there are going to be terrible events, if we can change the world, get everyone saved, do good and be good, can we slow down the timing of the Second Coming of Christ?"

The answer is *no*. The clock is set. HE IS COMING! No matter what! The very question itself, to slow down the coming of Christ, is demonic. Who would not want Jesus to come back besides Satan?

Beloved soldiers of Jesus, the Lord Jesus is counting on us to be on His side and obey His will. Together, with the firepower of heaven, we will put Satan down!

OPS BRIEFING 7

OPERATING FROM THE HEAVENLIES

The Lord's grace came on me one morning when I read Psalm 110. My heart was warmed with His presence, and I knew the Lord had graced me with insight into His ways of motivating the army of the Lord.

PSALM 110

The LORD *says to my Lord: "Sit at my right hand until I make your enemies a footstool for your feet."*

The LORD *will extend your mighty scepter from Zion; you will rule in the midst of your enemies.*

Your troops will be willing on your day of battle. Arrayed in holy majesty, from the womb of the dawn you will receive the dew of your youth.

The LORD *has sworn and will not change his mind: "You are a priest forever, in the order of Melchizedek."*

The Lord is at your right hand; he will crush kings on the day of his wrath.

He will judge the nations, heaping up the dead and crushing the rulers of the whole earth.

He will drink from a brook beside the way; therefore he will lift up his head.

As a soldier of the Lord, receive the briefings from the General of the Lord's Army, the Mighty Warrior (Exodus 15:3; Psalm 24:8; Revelation 19:11–21), the Commander in Chief, and the Defender (Proverbs 23:11).

SIT AT MY RIGHT HAND

In Bible language, the phrase *"sit at My right hand"* speaks of a position of honor and strength beside a king (Psalm 45:9; 1 Kings 2:19). You can say it as being enthroned to sit with Christ. To sit is also a position of authority and command, as in Psalm 2:4.

The anointing of the Lord is the strongest when you operate from a position of being seated in the presence of God. Being seated speaks of a rested position after the warfare has been accomplished. When a servant of God is "seated" with the Lord, it reveals much of his heart. He is a rested man in Christ.

My family went through a string of attacks from the enemy. Each family member experienced some form of setback. During this time, I was ministering in a church in Australia. The Holy Spirit placed in my heart to speak about spiritual warfare. The meeting was quite intense. I felt such heaviness in my heart throughout that trip. Some church meetings were even canceled due to problems within the churches.

When I returned to my hotel, my wife called and told me how our son had tripped as he was walking from the living room to the kitchen. He fell forward face-first and was bleeding from his mouth. My daughter was down with a fever, and my wife was facing unusual harassment from some of her nicest colleagues in the office.

I have served God long enough to know not to take circumstantial evidence as proof of spiritual warfare taking place, but when it occurs, you will know it is real spiritual warfare. And this was one of those red-alert moments. I returned home a week earlier from this trip with the intention to fast and pray for ten days to receive God's strength to stand firm and fight in the spirit realm.

On the first day of my fast, I began praising God with songs of worship. About an hour later, I heard the voice of Jesus. He directed me to Isaiah 40:1–2: "'Comfort, yes, comfort My people!' says your God. 'Speak comfort to Jerusalem, and cry out to her, that her warfare is ended…'" (NKJV).

The Lord directed me to rest in Him and to praise Him. He told me the warfare I was facing was already over, even before I started on the fast. This was just the last remaining residual attempt by the enemy to get me to doubt my victory in Christ.

I was glad the Lord spoke to me on the first day of my fast rather than on the last day. My fasting was over in a day. I rested in the Spirit to see the mighty hand of Jesus defending my family. There are times when we must learn to pray and prevail in the Spirit, and there are times we need to rest in the victory.

SEATED WITH CHRIST

EPHESIANS 2:6 AMPC

And He raised us up together with Him and made us sit down together [giving us joint seating with Him] in the heavenly sphere [by virtue of our being] in Christ Jesus (the Messiah, the Anointed One).

The truth of this revelation is this: When I learn to sit with Christ, He releases His authority in my life. Shake yourself free from the dust of worldliness, busyness, and hurriedness, and discipline your soul and body to sit down at His feet. It is a position of humility, the position of a disciple learning from the Master.

ISAIAH 52:2

Shake off your dust; rise up, sit enthroned, O Jerusalem. Free yourself from the chains on your neck, O captive Daughter of Zion.

Speaking of his personal experience in the life of intimacy with God and prayer, Henri Nouwen wrote, "In solitude I get rid of my scaffolding: no friends to talk with, no telephone calls to make, no meetings to attend, no music to entertain, no books to distract, just me—naked, vulnerable, weak, sinful, deprived, broken, nothing. It is this nothingness that I have to face in my solitude, a nothingness so dreadful that everything in me wants to run to my friends, my work, and my distractions so that I can forget my nothingness and make myself believe that I am worth something. As soon as I decide to stay in my solitude, confusing ideas, disturbing images, wild fantasies, and weird associations jump about in my mind like monkeys in a banana tree."[78]

In this position, our Lord will tutor us as His disciples. In this position, we are taught, refined, and transformed by the power of God through His Word and His Spirit. In this deeper walk, the Word of God becomes living and active, ever sharper than any double-edged sword, penetrating even to dividing the soul and spirit, joints and marrow; judging the thoughts and attitudes of the heart (Hebrews 4:12).

The Holy Spirit comes like fire and enters your heart to burn its contents, purifying it from impurities, as no ungodliness can endure the presence of a holy God. Everything becomes transparent and open before the eyes of the Lord, to whom we must give an account (Hebrews 4:13).

---

[78] Henri J.M. Nouwen, *The Way of the Heart: Desert Spirituality and Contemporary Ministry* (San Francisco: HarperSanFrancisco, 1981), 27–28.

Solitude is the furnace of transformation. Without solitude, we remain victims of our society, and we continue to be entangled in the illusions of false self.[79]

MALACHI 3:3

He will sit as a refiner and purifier of silver; he will purify the Levites and refine them like gold and silver. Then the Lord will have men who will bring offerings in righteousness.

In the secret place in your heart, the Lord, by His grace, enables you to be an overcomer (Revelation 3:21). Here, the Lord gives you the strength and the heart to let go of anything that prevents you from flowing in His will, no matter how hard and painful it may be (Hebrews 12:1).

The word *sit* comes from the Hebrew word *yashab*, meaning "to dwell, to remain, and to abide." One simple word, *sit*, opens a wide door of spiritual possibilities when acted upon and exercised with the right heart attitude in the presence of God.

When we study this word, *sit*, in the Hebrew language, this is the spiritual rule that stands out to the discerning: Where you sit spiritually makes a tremendous difference in your walk with God, and it affects everything else about you.

---

[79] Ibid., 25.

SIT IN GOD'S PRESENCE

PSALM 91:1 AMPC

He who dwells in the secret place of the Most High shall remain stable and fixed under the shadow of the Almighty [Whose power no foe can withstand].

PSALM 27:4 AMPC

One thing have I asked of the Lord, that will I seek, inquire for, and [insistently] require: that I may dwell in the house of the Lord [in His presence] all the days of my life, to behold and gaze upon the beauty [the sweet attractiveness and the delightful loveliness] of the Lord and to meditate, consider, and inquire in His temple.

PSALM 23:6 AMPC

Surely or only goodness, mercy, and unfailing love shall follow me all the days of my life, and through the length of my days the house of the Lord [and His presence] shall be my dwelling place.

Speaking of this silence of solitude in the presence of God, Brigid E. Herman, in her book, *Creative Prayer,* explained, "If we read the biographies of the great and wise, we shall find they were people of long silences and deep ponderings. Whatever of vision, of power, of genius there was in their work was wrought in silence. And when we turn to the inner circle of the spiritual masters—the men and women, not necessarily gifted or distinguished, to whom

God was a living, bright reality, which supernaturalized their everyday life and transmuted their homeliest actions into sublime worship—we find that their roots struck deep into the soil of spiritual silence."[80]

The word *yashab*, for *sit*, is also used for sitting in the gates, which speaks of deciding a case (Ruth 4:1–2; 1 Kings 22:10); sitting at the right hand, which speaks of a ruling position (Joel 3:12); and sitting in the dust or on the ground, which speaks of humiliation and grief (Isaiah 47:1).

Think of Peter; the gospel of Matthew tells us that "Peter followed him [Jesus] at a distance, right up to the courtyard of the high priest. He entered and sat down with the guards to see the outcome" (Matthew 26:58).

Beloved, it does matter with whom you are sitting in fellowship, as your associations will have a great influence on your soul. Peter was amid the persecutors of Christ, and that "ungodly" crowd denied his heart courage and faith. Instead, it placed fear in his soul.

PSALM 1:1–3 AMPC

Blessed (happy, fortunate, prosperous, and enviable) is the man who walks and lives not in the counsel of the ungodly [following their advice, their plans and purposes], nor stands [submissive and inactive] in the path where sinners

[80] Brigid E. Herman, *Creative Prayer* (New York: Harper and Row, n.d.), 31.

walk, nor sits down [to relax and rest] where the scornful [and the mockers] gather.

But his delight and desire are in the law of the Lord, and on His law (the precepts, the instructions, the teachings of God) he habitually meditates (ponders and studies) by day and by night.

And he shall be like a tree firmly planted [and tended] by the streams of water, ready to bring forth its fruit in its season; its leaf also shall not fade or wither; and everything he does shall prosper [and come to maturity].

The Bible commands us to sit at the right hand of Jesus until He makes His enemies our footstool. I believe this speaks of Jesus demonstrating His mighty power through your life and ministry. The demonic influences may try to block your path of progress in the divine will of God in the areas of your family, your physical health, your financial prosperity, your character, your integrity, and all that goes with honoring the name of Jesus on earth. God will back you up as you honor Him by sitting in His presence.

YOUR SCEPTER IS MIGHTY

2 CORINTHIANS 10:3–5 NLT

We are human, but we don't wage war as humans do.

We use God's mighty weapons, not worldly weapons, to knock down the strongholds of human reasoning and to destroy false arguments.

We destroy every proud argument that keeps people from knowing God. We capture their rebellious thoughts and teach them to obey Christ.

When you read about the life of David, you cannot help but marvel at his courage to trust and have faith that God would fulfill His promises to him and establish his family. As much as King Saul troubled David in the early days of his life, and with the enemies against whom David constantly had to fight to establish his reign, it was a known fact that the God of Israel fought for him.

In 2 Samuel 5:7–9, biblical history describes the conquests and the victories of David. Verse 10 reveals the secret of David's victory: "And he became more powerful, because the Lord God Almighty was with him." God established David's reign until no foe remained to stand before him.

This promise also speaks of the end of the age, when Jesus the King will establish His Kingdom on earth and when His enemies—Satan and his cohorts—will be cast into the depths of hell forever (Psalm 132:13–18; Revelation 19:20).

One point of consideration about the end-time prophecies in the book of Revelation is that these events had already taken place in time when God revealed them to John the Apostle. John reported what he saw as having already taken place. So, there is, in fact, no room for doubts as to whether or not these events will come to pass in the way the Bible predicts they will.

This same authority is available for you, fellow soldier of Christ. Only when you allow Jesus to rule your life will He use you to establish His Kingdom at every place the sole of your feet will tread. The extent to which you allow the in-workings of the Lord's rulership in your life is the extent to which His authority will manifest itself through your life and ministry.

No matter which situation you are in, God is for you. Cheer up!

The anointing will increase in proportion and capacity only for the one who learns to sit in the Lord's presence. The ministry of such a devoted disciple will be of substance and eternal value.

YOUR TROOPS MATTER TO GOD

PSALM 110:3

Your troops will be willing on your day of battle. Arrayed in holy majesty, from the womb of the dawn you will receive the dew of your youth.

As you keep in step with the divine counsel of God in conducting the affairs of your ministry, He will extend His command and supernatural influence over your troop, the people who are involved in your church and ministry. They will have a willing heart on the day of battle.

The Lord Jesus is preparing His Church for the final showdown. His Church will arise with power and might. The now seemingly weak in faith will be raised up by the mighty resurrection power of God, and they will become the giants in the faith (Joel 3:10). On the day of battle, these soldiers will be ready at the sound of the trumpet.

Dear servants of God, your people must be briefed about the battle strategies of the Lord. You are called to be God's spokesperson on this earth to teach His purposes on earth. The freshness of the Lord will leave your ministry if all that you care about is doing "a job." The Body of Christ must be taught their purposes—to establish the Kingdom of God on earth by saving souls and to build Jesus' Church. Their lives must become living sacrifices for the cause of God (Romans 12:1).

1 JOHN 3:8b AMPC

The reason the Son of God was made manifest (visible) was to undo (destroy, loosen, and dissolve) the works the devil [has done].

Jesus manifested the power of God and defeated the works of the enemy. His disciples did the same throughout the book of Acts. We have been given the same commissioning—to establish His Kingdom and destroy the works of the enemy (Matthew 28:18–20; Mark 16:17–18).

The Holy Spirit has already started His work of cleansing the house of the Lord and His people (1 Peter 4:17). The people of God have been warned by the Lord to raise the bar of holiness in their lives in comparison with this world (1 Peter 1:15–16). Stand up for the call of God. As His priest, be devoted to the Lord, and as a king, fight for the Lord and defend His Kingdom (Revelation 1:6).

The book of Revelation shows that there will be great battles fought in the end times and that our Lord Jesus Christ will defeat the enemy (Revelation 14:14–20; 16:12–16; 19:11–21; 20:7–10).

The Lord is already gathering His army all over this earth. His trumpet has sounded to servants of God all around (Joel 2:1, 15; Matthew 24:31). Like dew upon this earth, many will join the army of the Lord. The Body of Christ will win this final war!

This army will be raised up by the sole work of the Holy Spirit. Like David before Goliath, these will not want to use weapons of the flesh, nor will they follow the dictates of the spirit of religion (1 Samuel 17:38–40). Instead, they will walk in the Spirit, as taught by men who walk with God (Acts 4:13).

A strong apostolic mentoring is sweeping throughout the world. Many servants of God have been led by the Spirit to enter covenants of mentoring and discipleship. Like Paul, these servants will impart the ways of God to the Lord's army, who will then, in turn, take the world for Jesus.

OPS BRIEFING 8

THE INVISIBLE FORCE OF THE SUPERNATURAL COMPANY

It is the lack of secret prayer, the neglect of the maintenance of a hidden life "rooted and grounded in love," that explains the inability of the Christian life to resist the world and its failure to produce fruit abundantly. Nothing can change this except the restoration of the inner chamber in the life of the believer.

—Andrew Murray

Prayer is not the preparation for battle.
It is the battle.

—E. M. Bounds

There will be a restoration of the anointing of Elijah upon the Body of Christ as we eagerly await the coming of Christ. The principal anointing of prayer and boldness that was on Elijah will once again be poured upon the hungry child of God who desires to be used in this end-time visitation.

AN ANGEL VISITED ME

On November 9, 2004, my host in Sacramento, California, checked me into a hotel. I was scheduled to preach at the night service. After settling down and placing a cup of tea on the table, I opened my Bible to meditate on the text I intended to preach from that evening.

As my eyes beheld the pages of the Bible, the tip of my right ear burned hot, as though someone was pouring boiling oil over it. This tangible sensation lasted for almost half an hour. The presence of God flooded my soul. In the spirit, I saw an angel in my room, ready to deliver a divine message for the evening service. Although I have experienced such visitations in the past, this experience was unique.

The Scripture given to me was from 1 Peter 2:12: "on the day he visits us." I heard the voice of the Holy Spirit say, "God is laying a new burden upon this generation of people to cry out that God will visit them" (Micah 7:4). "God desires to make His Church strong and display His presence through her. She is the Lord's habitation" (Psalm 71:3).

EPHESIANS 2:22 KJV

In whom ye also are builded together for an habitation of God through the Spirit.

The Holy Spirit continued, "There is an angel of visitation for America that will pour out the purity of God. America will be cleansed." The Lord went on, "There must be an increase of prayer in the Church to set the house of the Lord in order; only then will much of the flesh and manipulation be gone. Righteousness and integrity will be established in the country. Come, My people, with fasting and prayer. Seek the Lord, and you will find Him."

I was reminded of the words of James 2:13: "Mercy triumphs over judgment." Our merciful, long-suffering, and patient God wants His people, His Church, to pray in intercession that His mercy will triumph in the midst of His judgment. The prophet Habakkuk echoed this prayer of mercy:

HABAKKUK 3:2 NLT

I have heard all about you, Lord. I am filled with awe by your amazing works.

In this time of our deep need, help us again as you did in years gone by. And in your anger, remember your mercy.

PSALM 78:38–39 AMPC

But He, full of [merciful] compassion, forgave their iniquity and destroyed them not; yes, many a time He turned His anger away and did not stir up all His wrath and indignation.

For He [earnestly] remembered that they were but flesh, a wind that goes and does not return.

In the context of the nature of God revealed in the Bible, it is biblical to understand that the mercy of God buys time from the execution of prevailing judgments. When the nation repents, judgment is lifted, and the mercy of God triumphs. When the nation does not repent, although repeated calls for repentance have been sounded, then the mercy of God makes way for the God-fearing people to escape the judgments that are to befall the nation. The mercy of God does not write off or cancel the judgments; rather, the mercy of God is the door of escape amid judgment.

This is the call of the Spirit to His Church at this critical hour of the Second Coming of Christ. The Church is to be the house of prayer to deliver the countless number of souls who are on their way to hell. The Church is the very womb that conceives the miracles of God and delivers the world that is hungering for the realm of the supernatural.

THE REALM OF THE SUPERNATURAL

The world is hungering for the realm of the supernatural. People are hungry to witness the supernatural power of God. They are hungry to know the will of God for their lives.

COLOSSIANS 1:9

For this reason, since the day we heard about you, we have not stopped praying for you and asking God to fill you with the knowledge of his will through all spiritual wisdom and understanding.

While different theological quarters of the Church are arguing over whether the gift of prophecy and the realm of the supernatural power of God are active today, millions of people are absorbed by the New Age Movement. The youth are more vulnerable as they are hungry for a tangible touch of God in their lives. They want God to take hold of them and lead them. They are crying out for the counsel of God to show them the way.

Unless the Body of Christ revisits her supernatural origin, we will lose millions of people at this finest hour. You cannot deny the miracles or His miraculous interventions in the course of the history of mankind in which He accomplishes His purposes.

This is the hour when we will witness the power of God descending and making human history again. We will witness the days of Moses, when God showed Himself as the all-powerful One. Many theologians who do not believe in miracles, and those who have spent their entire lives writing books "proving" that God has done away with His power, are going to have the shock of their lives as they witness this supernatural move of God.

Church, you are called to be the warrior-bride for the King! I see the Lord Jesus standing up from His heavenly throne, ready to execute His purposed will on the earth. Do not be left behind with the doubters, but stand among the company of faith and execute the works of God.

THE SUPERNATURAL COMPANY

The company of Elijah will be trained by God to flow in the realm of the supernatural. It will be a primary nature for this company to minister in the Spirit. They will have the power to bring every thought captive to the obedience of Christ. Hallelujah! The Church must walk in this realm of authority in these last days, when more than ever before, demons are dragging souls to hell with counterfeit power.

2 CORINTHIANS 10:4–5 AMPC

For the weapons of our warfare are not physical [weapons of flesh and blood], but they are mighty before God for the overthrow and destruction of strongholds,

[Inasmuch as we] refute arguments and theories and reasonings and every proud and lofty thing that sets itself up against the [true] knowledge of God; and we lead every thought and purpose away captive into the obedience of Christ (the Messiah, the Anointed One).

SUPERNATURAL EYESIGHT

2 Kings 6:15–17

When the servant of the man of God got up and went out early the next morning, an army with horses and chariots had surrounded the city. "Oh, my lord, what shall we do?" the servant asked.

"Don't be afraid," the prophet answered. "Those who are with us are more than those who are with them."

And Elisha prayed, "O LORD, open his eyes so he may see." Then the LORD opened the servant's eyes, and he looked and saw the hills full of horses and chariots of fire all around Elisha.

In order to operate in the realm of the supernatural, we must walk in a deeper level of the Spirit, where our spiritual eyes are opened to see the demonstrations of God. It is then that the activity of heaven becomes real and tangible to us.

Can you imagine what a contrast it was for Gehazi, the servant of Elisha? With natural eyes, he saw an army with horses and chariots surrounding the city and fear struck him, but with the eyes of the Spirit, he saw the hills full of horses and chariots of fire all around Elisha. It pays to be a servant of the man of God! You get to see the supernatural!

The army that God is raising up through the spirit of prayer will be enabled to see in the supernatural. This was the heartfelt prayer of Paul for the Ephesian church.

EPHESIANS 1:17–18 AMPC

[For I always pray to] the God of our Lord Jesus Christ, the Father of glory, that He may grant you a spirit of wisdom and revelation [of insight into mysteries and secrets] in the [deep and intimate] knowledge of Him, by having the eyes of your heart flooded with light, so that you can know and understand the hope to which He has called you, and how rich is His glorious inheritance in the saints (His set-apart ones).

When the spirit of revelation opens the eyes of your heart, the light of heaven floods your soul, causing you to know and understand the things pertaining to heaven and its priorities.

Our Lord Jesus constantly operated with such supernatural eyesight that He declared in John 5:19, "I tell you the truth, the Son can do nothing by himself; he can do only what he sees his Father doing, because whatever the Father does the Son also does."

It is this gift that gives us supernatural understanding in the workings of God and reveals the secret plans of Satan against the people of God. It is this supernatural eyesight that brought understanding to John when he saw the events of the book of Revelation unfold before him. It is this supernatural eyesight that gave the spirit of boldness to the servants of God in the Bible. Think of Moses. On the one side, he saw the armies of Pharaoh with his chariots right behind the children of Israel, and yet on the other side, he saw the angel of the Lord and the pillar of cloud defending them (Exodus 14:19–20).

NO COUNTERFEIT CAN STAND BEFORE GOD

In 1 Kings 18:16–40, we read of Elijah's greatest moment in history. God honored him as a prophet of the Most High in the midst of the prophets of Baal. In such moments in history, a servant of God will know how much God stands with him when every word that comes from his mouth is fulfilled.

That event in the Bible was the biggest showdown in the history of King Ahab and Jezebel. It ticked her off. Elijah wanted to set the record straight once and for all. He had endured enough of Jezebel's control, intimidation, verbal abuse, and challenges to "whose God is bigger" (1 Kings 18:21). Having assembled over 450 prophets of Baal and 400 prophets of Asherah, Elijah prepared the altar and asked the people to place bull's meat on it. He then got them to pour water on the sides of the altar. The God who brings down fire from heaven and licks up the waters from the altar wins (1 Kings 18:30–38). What gameplay! Elijah went on to mock the prophets of Baal and Asherah as they cut themselves to sacrifice the blood from their own bodies and as they chanted the names of their gods all day long.

1 KINGS 18:26–29

So they took the bull given them and prepared it. Then they called on the name of Baal from morning till noon. "O Baal, answer us!" they shouted. But there was no response; no one answered. And they danced around the altar they had made. At noon Elijah began to taunt them. "Shout louder!" he said. "Surely he is a god! Perhaps he is deep in thought, or busy, or traveling. Maybe he is sleeping and must be awakened." So they shouted louder and slashed themselves with swords and spears, as was their custom, until their blood flowed. Midday passed, and they continued their frantic prophesying until the time for the evening sacrifice. But there was no response, no one answered, no one paid attention.

The phrase "*as was their custom*" reveals that the false prophets had performed their usual rituals, and their god usually showed up. However, this one time, something was off, and the false prophets did not know why.

Beloved, the answer is clear for us. Which demon would dare to stand before the God of Elijah? Which demon in hell would dare take on the challenge to stand in the boxing ring with our Lord Jesus?

When the demons realized who their Challenger was they did not show up. That is the God of Elijah! No counterfeit can stand before the true works of Jesus. What gave Elijah that stone-headed boldness? The Bible says he acted in obedience to the instructions of God (v. 36).

Supernatural power is made available to the obedient and the prayerful. To the one who prays, God speaks. To the one who prays, God shows up. To the one who prays, God reveals.

A similar type of encounter is seen in Exodus 7:10–13, when Moses was challenged by the sorcerers of Pharaoh. Only this time, Moses, who was sent by the true, living God, won the contest!

THE DOUBLE-EDGED SWORD OF PRAYER AND THE WORD

1 KINGS 19:18

Yet I reserve seven thousand in Israel—all whose knees have not bowed down to Baal and all whose mouths have not kissed him.

God told Elijah that the company He had reserved consisted of those whose knees had not bowed down to Baal and all whose mouths had not yet kissed him. This seems to be a quality that stood out in them, and God had been dealing with them to qualify them to be part of this company. Our Lord Jesus pays attention to the hearts of ministers and the quality of the fruit they bear for the Kingdom of God. Each of us must pay careful attention to conduct ministry in the will of God, as any works of the flesh will be written off (1 Corinthians 3:10–15).

Elijah carried the seal of heaven's quality when he said, "As the LORD of hosts lives, before whom I stand" (1 Kings 18:15 NKJV). This was the secret of Elijah's boldness. This was the secret of Elijah's ministry. He was a man who stood before God. He was a man who spent time in communion with Him.

THE BENDED KNEES

One of the remarkable hallmarks of the end-time army of warriors must be their prayer life. This army knows how to pray and possess the victory. This was the quality that made the disciples stand above the religious leaders of their days. The early church disciples prayed and prayed, and they kept on praying.

ACTS 4:13 AMPC

Now when they saw the boldness and unfettered eloquence of Peter and John and perceived that they were unlearned and untrained in the schools [common men with no educational advantages], they marveled; and they recognized that they had been with Jesus.

The band of twelve disciples just wanted to spend more time in prayer and the Word (Acts 6:4). They were identified as men who had been with Jesus. The fellowships they organized were saturated in prayer and devotion to God (Acts 2:43–47; 4:23–31).

After this order, the early Christian band of believers was formed. They were of solid mold, preachers of the heavenly type, heroic, stalwart, soldierly, and saintly. Preaching for them meant self-denying, self-crucifying, serious, toilsome, and martyr-type business.[81]

THE SPIRIT OF FERVENCY

Fervent prayer produces fervent soldiers for the cause of God. No one can be fervent for God without being fervent in the closet, on one's knees before God.

---

81 E.M. Bounds, *The Complete Works of E.M. Bounds* (Grand Rapids, Mich., 1990), 449.

JAMES 5:16b, 17–18 AMPC

The earnest (heartfelt, continued) prayer of a righteous man makes tremendous power available [dynamic in its working].

Elijah was a human being with a nature such as we have [with feelings, affections, and a constitution like ours]; and he prayed earnestly for it not to rain, and no rain fell on the earth for three years and six months.

And [then] he prayed again and the heavens supplied rain and the land produced its crops [as usual].

Reverend E.M. Bounds paraphrased James 5:16–18 in this way: "See what prayer can do, by Elijah! Pray as Elijah prayed. Let the righteous man put forth to its fullest extent the energy of prayer. Let saints and sinners, angels and devil, see and feel the mighty potencies of prayer. See how the prayer of a good man has power and influence, and avails with God."[82]

When the Holy Spirit showed me this passage in the church, He emphasized the prayer of persistence and fervency as the urgent need of the hour. This company whom the Lord is raising up must know and will know how to pray through. Their prayer lives will touch heaven, rock the world, and wreck hell! These men and women's knees will only bow to Jesus and not to any religious leaders. Their allegiance is to Christ and His cause and not to the personal visions of men.

---

[82] Ibid., 513.

ROMANS 12:11 KJV

Not slothful in business; fervent in spirit; serving the Lord.

The word *fervent* comes from a Greek word, *zeo*, meaning "to be hot and boiling in spirit." From this same word, we get the words *agony* and *to strive for* in prayer (Colossians 4:12). In 2 Corinthians 7:7, the noun *zelos*, or "zeal," is translated as "fervent mind."

Dr. Vine, in his famous *Expository Dictionary of Biblical Words*, noted, "There is nothing in the original corresponding to the word 'effectual.' The phrase, including the verb '*energeomai*,' meaning 'to work in,' is lit., 'the inworking supplication,' which suggests a supplication consistent with inward conformity to the mind of God."[83]

Elijah was a man fervent in prayer and consistent, too. The Apostle James noted that Elijah prayed "again." This quality of being "hooked to" a God-type of prayer is the missing element in the present-day church. We are willing to wait for everything else in the world except to wait upon God. When you must wait for seven days to receive a response for an application, it may seem acceptable. However, to wait upon the Lord for seven days to receive a response may seem a waste of time.

God wants warmhearted servants. The Holy Spirit comes as a fire to dwell in us. We are to be baptized with the Holy Spirit and with fire. Fervency is the warmth of the soul. If our faith does not set us on fire, it is because we have frozen hearts. Our prayers must be red-hot. Coldness of spirit hinders our prayers. Prayer

---

83 *Vine's Expository Dictionary of New Testament Words*, (Nashville: Thomas Nelson, 1985).

cannot live in a wintry atmosphere. Chilly surroundings freeze out petitioning and dry up the springs of supplication.[84]

My fellow comrades in the Lord's army, you cannot conduct spiritual warfare in an "air-conditioned" room. There is no such thing as warfare without sweat. When the Church prays important and urgent prayers that are of heavenly importance in a cold and casual manner, you know she is not warring in the Spirit. She is just playing war games.

Real praying with the power of the Holy Spirit is full of energy, agony, and sweat. You can be in a cold, air-conditioned room, yet your body will be full of heat as the fire of the Holy Spirit engulfs your prayer and your entire being. It is in this type of prayer mode that your natural mind is suspended, and the eyes of your spirit are opened to heavenly realities. It is in this type of prayer that the Lord Jesus releases His angels to surround you and assist you in ushering your heavenly cries to the throne of God (Revelation 8:3–4).

It is through this type and time of prayer that you are energized by the fire of the Holy Spirit, and you become hotter than the fires of hell. No demon in hell will ever dare to come near or block the pathway of your prayer from rising to the throne of His mercy.

God is looking for bended knees! The application is still wide open for whoever wants to sign up to become a prayer warrior and join the ranks of His invisible force. We need fresh fire from heaven to fall upon the Church.

---

[84] E.M. Bounds, *The Complete Works of E.M. Bounds* (Grand Rapids, Mich.: Baker Books, 1990), 35.

"The fire of the Holy Spirit brings power.

Never mind the noise. Let us apply this power to get on the move. The proper purpose of Pentecost is to get the wheels rolling for God in every church, thereby transporting the Gospel across the face of the earth."

—Reinhard Bonnke

THE MINISTRY OF TEARS

One of the prophecies the Lord gave me while I was fasting and praying in December 1998 was this: "Weeping prophets like Jeremiah are going to be restored in the Church. A dry-eyed Church cannot serve Me." Unless we take hold of the horns of the altar of God and pray in intercession, nothing much will happen to effect lasting results in our lives and ministries. The ministry of intercession has always been the key denominator in all the moves of God throughout biblical and contemporary Church history.

Pay attention now—I am not saying that you must always pray in tears; neither am I saying that unless you pray with tears, your prayers will not be answered. I am saying there is an army of prayer warriors whom the Lord is raising up who will pray and travail with tears. We should not be embarrassed nor shame others who are fervent in prayer with tears.

Job prayed with tears (Job 16:20). David prayed with tears (Psalm 56:8). The Prophet Jeremiah was known for his ministry of prayer with tears (Jeremiah 9:1; Lamentations 2:18). The Apostle Paul served the Lord with humility and tears (Acts 20:19). The shortest verse in the Bible reads, "Jesus wept" (John 11:35), and while on His earthly mission, Jesus prayed with strong cries and tears (Hebrews 5:7).

In the Bible, the life of a prophet is often associated with the ministry of tears. Nehemiah wept over Jerusalem (Nehemiah 1:4). Those who carry the watchman anointing, like Ezekiel, will often be found in prayer and tears. In Bible history, a prophet is often known for his prayer and intimacy with God rather than his prophecies. Leonard Ravenhill said, "The great revivalists were all great reapers in public because they were weepers in private."

Your closeness with Jesus will ensure the sharing of His burdens to your heart. You will experience supernatural interference—the Holy Spirit will bring a person or some urgency of someone in your heart for whom you must intercede. You may be burdened to pray for a country that you have not been to or for a people group that you have not met.

"In prayer, I must wrestle like Jacob, and pant like David, and hope like Elijah, and be persistent like Bartimaeus, and cry with tears like my blessed Lord," said Alexander Smellie.

THE INVISIBLE FORCE OF PREVAILING, PERSISTENT PRAYER

Prevailing prayer is God's ordained means for extending His Kingdom, for defeating Satan and his empire of darkness and evil, and for fulfilling God's eternal plan and bringing into effect His good and perfect will on the earth. Prevailing prayer is God's prioritized strategy. The history of the Church can never be fully written until Christ in eternity reveals the mighty hidden prayer involvement of all His praying people.[85]

1 KINGS 18:41–44

And Elijah said to Ahab, "Go, eat and drink, for there is the sound of a heavy rain."

So Ahab went off to eat and drink, but Elijah climbed to the top of Carmel, bent down to the ground and put his face between his knees. "Go and look toward the sea," he told his servant. And he went up and looked. "There is nothing there," he said. Seven times Elijah said, "Go back."

The seventh time the servant reported, "A cloud as small as a man's hand is rising from the sea." So Elijah said, "Go and tell Ahab, 'Hitch up your chariot and go down before the rain stops you.'"

It is rather interesting to note the different times Elijah prayed for the spectacular display of God's wonders and how long it took him to pray. During a course of conversation with Ahab, Elijah commanded the rain to stop (1 Kings 17:1). There was no evidence of prayer. Then why did God answer?

---

[85] Wesley L. Duewel. *Mighty Prevailing Prayer* (Grand Rapids, Mich.: Zondervan, 1990), 13.

MATTHEW 6:6 AMPC

But when you pray, go into your [most] private room, and, closing the door, pray to your Father, Who is in secret; and your Father, Who sees in secret, will reward you in the open.

The answer lies in his secret lifestyle of prayer. God made Elijah in the secret place. No one knew him. Nobody knew where he came from. He was the secret missile of heaven that was waiting to be launched on earth. There were no records of Elijah before 1 Kings 17. He came and he commanded, and it stopped raining for three years. This man was shaped by God as he prayed and travailed before Him. For Elijah, prayer and travail were synonymous. Just observe the way he prayed on Mount Carmel. He "bent down to the ground and put his head between his knees." That can only be done by someone who knows how to pray on bended knee!

In 1 Kings 18:36–37, Elijah prayed possibly for less than a minute. God answered him by fire from heaven. It was that quick. Can you just visualize the look on the faces of the false prophets?

Sometimes what seems like a simple, instant answer to prayer can be the crowning climax of days and months, or even years, of faithful intercession.[86]

However, on top of Mount Carmel, Elijah had to pray seven times. What went wrong? Was God displeased with Elijah? Was he not in God's will anymore? Was some sin blocking his prayer? These are the usual thought patterns of any one of us who is serious

---

[86] Wesley L. Duewel. *Mighty Prevailing Prayer* (Grand Rapids, Mich.: Zondervan, 1990), 16.

about practicing prevailing prayer. But again, there was no evidence of such an internal struggle in Elijah at all.

LUKE 18:1 AMPC

Also [Jesus] told them a parable to the effect that they ought always to pray and not to turn coward (faint, lose heart, and give up).

Beloved, here again is the divine lesson in the school of prevailing prayer. Pray until the answer comes. Do not let your mind, your circumstances, or the devil confuse you on the length of time it is taking; rather, submit yourself and the pressing situation into the hands of God until the answer comes from heaven. The Lord will command His angels to hold your situation together and keep it from falling apart.

In the midst of possible discouragement and in an impossible situation, Elijah did not doubt whether or not a miracle would happen. He kept on praying. He persisted until he saw heaven responding to his prayer. Prevail in prayer until the Holy Spirit releases His grip on you, until you receive an assurance within that heaven has heard your voice, until you secure the grace and the mercy of God on the situation.

We are standing at the threshold of Jesus' Second Coming. Unless we prevail in prayer, filled with the Holy Spirit and fire, the company of the overcomers cannot move forward.

We must prevail in prayer for situations in which God's will is thwarted and where Satan is delaying and blocking Christ's cause.

We must prevail for lives that are ensnared and blinded by sin, as they are unable or unwilling to pray for themselves.[87]

Dr. Wesley Duewel, in his book, *Mighty Prevailing Prayer,* has listed seven levels of prevailing prayer. I want to encourage you to get this book, devour the pages in the Spirit, and practice the principles on your knees.

LEVELS OF PREVAILING PRAYER[88]

Level 1: Ask—Matthew 7:7

Level 2: Seek—The asking becomes longer and more intensive.

Level 3: Knock—Interceding becomes even more urgent and insistent.

Level 4: Fast—To the precious crescendo of intensity and urgency of intercession, fasting is added.

Level 5: Prayer Burden—The burden may be intense and brief, or perhaps it extends over a longer period of time.

Level 6: Wrestling in Prayer—Very intense praying

Level 7: Prayer Warfare—Prayer battle, extending over a prolonged period of time

---

87 Wesley L. Duewel. *Mighty Prevailing Prayer* (Grand Rapids, Mich.: Zondervan, 1990), 15.

88 Ibid., 16.

HOLY SPIRIT–EMPOWERED PRAYERS

ROMANS 8:26–27 AMPC

So too the [Holy] Spirit comes to our aid and bears us up in our weakness; for we do not know what prayer to offer nor how to offer it worthily as we ought, but the Spirit Himself goes to meet our supplications and pleads in our behalf with unspeakable yearnings and groanings too deep for utterance. And He Who searches the hearts of men knows what is in the mind of the [Holy] Spirit [what His intent is], because the Spirit intercedes and pleads [before God] in behalf of the saints according to and in harmony with God's will.

The Lord Jesus is not expecting His followers in His Church to battle on their knees by themselves. Prayer, unless it is guided and led by the Spirit, cannot penetrate through the enemy lines. We need the Holy Spirit to teach us. He knows exactly how to pray according to the mind of the Father. The Holy Spirit always guides us to pray accurately, according to the will of God.

Daniel was on his knees, fasting and praying to gain understanding of the vision that he saw. It seemed like he had been praying forever. Daniel did not know the reason for the delay, but he kept on praying and pressing forward in the Spirit. An angel appeared to him and revealed that God had commanded the angel to give Daniel "air support" as the prince of Persia was resisting and had delayed the answer for twenty-one days (Daniel 10:12–13).

Prayers that are prayed in our limited natural strength cannot get the job done. Weak, ineffective, timid prayers will not get the job done. Don't think for a moment that the spiritual forces of darkness, keeping untold thousands in your city in bondage to drugs, alcohol, sexual perversion, lust, greed, and every other form of sin, will lose their hold according to prayers that are prayed in any man's natural strength.[89]

In our own natural understanding, we cannot know or recognize the evil principalities and powers that have established strongholds in our communities, cities, or nations. We cannot face these principalities only with head knowledge! It takes spiritual discernment through the Holy Spirit to expose the evil principalities, and it takes power and authority flowing through us in prayer to demolish their strongholds.[90]

Prayer is just one plan in God's grand strategy. Evangelism is essential in spiritual warfare. Casting out Satan is a victory thrown away unless followed up with a full-on Gospel assault. Otherwise, Satan will reoccupy the position (Luke 11:26). The Gospel is an explosive force, but it needs the detonator of prayer. Prayer, however, has nothing to detonate without the preached Gospel. That is the outline of divine strategy.

First, there must be a prayer bombardment against the entrenchment of the enemy, and then the infantry goes in with

89 Morris Cerullo, *The Last Great Anointing* (Ventura, Calif.: Renew, Gospel Light, 1999), 134.

90 Ibid., 140.

the Gospel-witnessing battalions armed with the Word of God in hand, ready to take captives and occupy the position.[91]

SMALL, YOU SAY? IT'S JUST THE START!

It is through this type of prevailing prayer that we will witness the display of God's power and manifestation in the affairs of our lives and nations. Sometimes the answer could be small, but it is just the beginning.

Each time Elijah sent his servant to check whether the clouds were forming to rain, in answer to his prevailing prayer, six times the answer was the same: "There is nothing there." Did Elijah get discouraged? No, I don't think so. He kept on praying. Through years of travailing in prayer, he knew that sometimes it just takes time for some miracles to happen. He pressed on.

The fire of the Holy Spirit has started to fall once again. The spirit of prayer is catching on in many churches across the nations. More knees are bowing to pray at the same time, more so than ever before. The rain clouds are forming. The sound of prevailing prayer is rising from earth to heaven.

Church, let us keep on praying. The rain of the Lord will come in, pouring, greater in density than the power of a tsunami. Pastors, this is not the time to mourn over your small congregation. Perhaps you are in a small town. Nobody may know you or your powerful ministry. Praise God! You are kept hidden and

---

[91] Reinhard Bonnke, *Evangelism by Fire* (Germany: Full Flame GmbH, 2001), 278–279.

undisturbed by casual Christianity so that you can concentrate on matters pertaining to the Kingdom and pray.

As your church prays, clouds will form over your church. These few raindrops are just the beginning of the revival fire that will sweep through your town because you obeyed and prayed. God will speak to you supernaturally.

My brother, Sadhu Sundar Selvaraj, a man of fasting and prevailing prayer, always admonishes people to pay attention to the handwriting on the wall (Daniel 5:5). There is always a message the Lord will convey to His children. These are the "secret codes" of the leading of the Holy Spirit as we wait upon Him for direction.

SUPERNATURAL PLACEMENTS

> **1 KINGS 18:46**
>
> *The power of the LORD came upon Elijah and, tucking his cloak into his belt, he ran ahead of Ahab all the way to Jezreel.*

I believe there is a global supernatural placement by God. The Lord is moving His people around to occupy strategic locations and positions to serve Him before the coming of Jesus. The Lord is moving His apostles and prophets to strategic locations to prepare the remnant. In 2019, the Lord Jesus spoke to me in a heavenly encounter to move from Singapore to North Carolina, USA. He gave me the address of the property I must buy and directed me to buy a church property. He gave me the date by which I must place my foot in the land. My wife and I obeyed the voice of God and left everything behind in Singapore, and came to our promised land.

We planted a church during the Covid-19 pandemic. We ministered to many, and today the church is growing, touching hundreds of lives in live service and thousands online. The testimony of this apostolic move itself deserves another book.

Through the power of the Holy Spirit, Elijah ran faster than the chariot of Ahab. He was supernaturally energized to be in Jezreel. This was also the experience of Philip in Acts 8:39, where the Holy Spirit suddenly took him away after he had baptized the eunuch. Mordecai sent word to Esther: "For if you remain silent at this time, relief and deliverance for the Jews will arise from another place, but you and your father's family will perish. And who knows but that you have come to royal position for such a time as this?" (Esther 4:14).

In the same manner, the Lord is supernaturally placing many Esthers, Daniels, and Josephs in key positions in society for His cause. The Lord has hidden His men. They are not in position yet. We should not get too distressed at the present political state of the nations and wonder about the future. As we pray, the hand of God will move.

THE SWORD OF THE SPIRIT

1 KINGS 19:18

"Yet I reserve seven thousand in Israel—all whose knees have not bowed down to Baal and all whose mouths have not kissed him."

The other required divine quality of end-time warriors is the Word of God in their mouths. The Lord wants His people to keep their mouths and their words pure so they can be used as anointed weapons against the camp of the enemy. The Word of God has the capability to destroy the enemy's assaults. Only those who have taken time to mature and grow in the Word and Spirit will be effective and cause great damage to the kingdom of darkness.

Elijah's life of obedience to God was lived out in a higher level of authority, such that he was able to declare, "As the LORD God of Israel lives, before whom I stand, there shall not be dew nor rain these years, except at my word" (1 Kings 17:1 NKJV). Such an authority came forth when he said, "except at my word."

The religious leaders and the people who came to hear the message of Jesus also declared, "He taught as one who had authority, and not as their teachers of the law" (Matthew 7:29). The Bible says that God displayed His power and confirmed the Word the disciples preached (Mark 16:20). Paul wrote in 1 Corinthians 2:4: "And my speech and my preaching were not with persuasive words of human wisdom, but in demonstration of the Spirit and of power" (NKJV).

Dear soldier in the Lord's army, spend quality time with the Word of God, in meditation, and in study. Sharpen your spirit by practicing the Word in your life. You see, Satan fears practicing Christians and those who walk in the ways of God. He is least bothered by those who just listen but do not cause real damage to the works of darkness.

THE WORD IS A WEAPON

EPHESIANS 6:13–18 NKJV

Therefore take up the whole armor of God, that you may be able to withstand in the evil day, and having done all, to stand. Stand therefore, having girded your waist with truth, having put on the breastplate of righteousness, and having shod your feet with the preparation of the gospel of peace; above all, taking the shield of faith with which you will be able to quench all the fiery darts of the wicked one. And take the helmet of salvation, and the sword of the Spirit, which is the word of God; praying always with all prayer and supplication in the Spirit, being watchful to this end with all perseverance and supplication for all the saints.

THE BELT OF TRUTH

Paul mentioned in verse 14 that we are to "stand therefore, having girded your waist with truth" (NKJV). The word *truth* is to be understood as the truth of the Gospel (Romans 1:25). The Word of God is the Truth (John 14:6; 17:17). The King James Version translates this as: "loins girt about with truth." The belt is the invisible defensive piece of the armor of the Roman soldier. Only he can feel it; it cannot be seen by anyone else.

The dictionary defines *loins* as the region of the hips, groin, lower abdomen, and reproductive organs. If, in the natural, it is important to the human body, is it then any less important in the spiritual life, as Paul compares the truth of God's Word to our loins?

When we faithfully sow the seed of the truth into our lives, only then will we bear fruit for the Kingdom of God (John 15:2–4; 1 John 3:9). The time you spend in the Word may not be visible to anyone else, but you alone will know it in your heart. This is the invisible cover of God's protection over your life.

There are too many casual Christians in the Church today. They don't have time to study the Word, not to mention praying. Casual Christians are cold Christians. Cold prayers do not carry enough heat to warm their own souls, much less bring or receive answers from heaven.

JOB 23:12

I have not departed from the commands of his lips; I have treasured the words of his mouth more than my daily bread.

Store the Word in your life (Deuteronomy 6:6; Proverbs 4:20). Hiding the Word within your heart is the secret to purity and walking right before the Lord. The Word gives you strength and protection from the wiles of the enemy (Psalm 119:9–11). The Word produces the divine healing balm to the body of those who will hold it sacred in their hearts (Proverbs 4:20–22). The Word will bring success to all areas of your life and make you to shine wherever you are in the world (Joshua 1:8; Psalm 1:3).

THE SWORD OF THE SPIRIT

Another offensive weapon made available to the child of God is the sword of the Spirit. Paul used the Greek word *machaira* for "sword," denoting a deadly weapon that Roman soldiers used in close combat. Both edges of the sword were razor-sharp.

The sword of the Spirit is the Word of God. Here, "word" is translated from the Greek word *rhema*, which simply means the inspired and quickened Word of the Lord. The Lord considers His Word to be highly effective and dangerous against the demonic hosts.

That's why the enemy will do everything he can to get the Word out of your life!

The written Word of God, when stored in your heart, will become an inspired word for your situation. The Holy Spirit will draw the stored Scriptures from your heart and give you the right word for the moment. He knows how to counterattack the works of the enemy, and He knows how to prepare His people before an attack comes.

When you have a lack of the Word in your heart, the Holy Spirit has nothing much to draw from. That is why many people feel they have no leading from the Lord, and their hearts remain devoid of the counsel of the Holy Spirit.

COLOSSIANS 3:16 AMPC

Let the word [spoken by] Christ (the Messiah) have its home [in your hearts and minds] and dwell in you in [all its] richness, as you teach and admonish and train one another in all insight and intelligence and wisdom [in spiritual things, and as you sing] psalms and hymns and spiritual songs, making melody to God with [His] grace in your hearts.

Take heed to the admonishments of the Scriptures, and let the Word of God dwell in you with all its richness. Nevertheless, be aware that the enemy fights you when you store the Word in your heart. Imagine if a police officer were to spot you with a sword by your side. You are a potential danger. You would be arrested immediately. So it is in the spiritual realm!

This happened to Elijah. He constantly had the Word of the Lord in him. He had a reputation in Israel for being a troubler of Israel (1 Kings 18:17)! You are a potential threat to the kingdom of darkness when you carry the *rhema* word in your life.

That is why Satan will fight the prophets and prophetic churches. They carry the Word of the Lord to this generation. Jezebel hates the prophets. She knows that she cannot win against the prophets of God and the anointed Church.

A PHYSICAL ENCOUNTER WITH A DEMON

I remember one incident that took place in the year 2002. I was scheduled to preach at a church in Australia. The Holy Spirit spoke to me that I should speak on the subject of Jezebel and her attacks against the Church. I would rather talk about anything else in the Bible than this type of heavy subject. But when the Lord chooses the subject, He always has a reason as to why He wants to speak to that particular church on that particular subject. I submitted to His leading, prepared myself in the evening, prayed, and then went to bed.

In the middle of the night, Jezebel appeared in my room. Though my body was sleeping, my spirit saw her, and I heard her voice. She warned me not to preach about her in the church. She told me that if I did, there would be dire consequences. There was a strong tug-of-war that took place in the Spirit. She harassed my physical body. My entire body was moving and felt the strain. I prayed in the Spirit, and moments later, the authority of God rose up within me, and I commanded her to leave in Jesus' name.

The next morning when I woke up, I realized I had strained my neck in the warfare. Nevertheless, I did preach the message in the church, and there was a great deliverance. Many responded to the altar call, and many repented before the Lord.

THE DOUBLE-EDGED SWORD

REVELATION 1:16 NASB

In His right hand He held seven stars, and out of His mouth came a sharp two-edged sword; and His face was like the sun shining in its strength.

On the island of Patmos, John saw a vision of Jesus in His glory and power. John saw a double-edged sword coming forth from His mouth.

The word "two-edged" comes from the Greek word *distomos*, meaning "two-mouthed." The same Greek word is used in Hebrews 4:12 for the Word of God, and also in Revelation 2:12.

HEBREWS 4:12 AMPC

For the Word that God speaks is alive and full of power [making it active, operative, energizing, and effective]; it is sharper than any two-edged sword, penetrating to the dividing line of the breath of life (soul) and [the immortal] spirit, and of joints and marrow [of the deepest parts of our nature], exposing and sifting and analyzing and judging the very thoughts and purposes of the heart.

Dear comrades, do not underestimate the power of revelation in your life. It is like walking with fully loaded weapons. Anytime the Holy Spirit calls on you, you are ready to fight.

Understand this: The Word has been spoken by Jesus, and the Bible has recorded it (2 Timothy 3:16). Now, this same Word stored in your heart, when spoken by the power of the Holy Spirit, is like dynamite working through you. This causes massive destruction to the kingdom of darkness.

First, the mouth of the Lord has spoken, and now the Holy Spirit wants you to speak the inspired Word from your mouth. It then becomes a two-mouthed, two-edged sword. It is no longer your sword; it has now become the sword of the Spirit. Amen!

ISAIAH 55:11 AMPC

So shall My word be that goes forth out of My mouth: it shall not return to Me void [without producing any effect, useless], but it shall accomplish that which I please and purpose, and it shall prosper in the thing for which I sent it.

THE COMING SPECIAL FORCE COMMANDOS

REVELATION 11:3–6

"And I will give power to my two witnesses, and they will prophesy for 1,260 days, clothed in sackcloth." These are the two olive trees and the two lampstands that stand before the Lord of the earth. If anyone tries to harm them, fire comes from their mouths and devours their enemies. This is how anyone who wants to harm them must die. These men have power to shut up the sky so that it will not rain during the time they are prophesying; and they have power to turn the waters into blood and to strike the earth with every kind of plague as often as they want.

The coming end-time warriors of heaven are going to carry this two-edged sword. They are heaven's knights who will personally confront the Antichrist. Their ministry is of great value during the Tribulation.

THE IDENTITY OF THE TWO WITNESSES

Some Bible commentators identify these two witnesses as Elijah and Moses, based on their past ministry records. Elijah's record showed him calling down fire from heaven (2 Kings 1:10) and commanding the rain to stop (1 Kings 17:1). Moses' record showed water being turned into blood and him commanding plagues to come upon the Egyptians (Exodus 7:14; 11:10). Others say these two witnesses will be Enoch and Elijah, as neither of them died physically while on the earth, for God "took them away" (Genesis 5:24; 2 Kings 2:11). Enoch also saw the Second Coming of Christ in a vision (Jude 1:14–15). The Bible says, "It is appointed for men to die once" (Hebrews 9:27 NKJV). Who among these men will come again?

There is a possible clue found in Revelation 11:4: that these two witnesses are the two olive trees and two lampstands that stand before the Lord of the earth. This is quoted from Zechariah 4:3, 11, and 14, in which Zerubbabel and Joshua, the high priest, were the leaders of Israel in Zechariah's time. This means, then, that these two witnesses must be Israelites. Enoch was a Gentile who lived before the Abrahamic Covenant took place; therefore, he may not be a probable candidate.

THEIR MINISTRY

These two men will be so mightily anointed by the Holy Spirit that their ministries this time, as mentioned in Revelation 11, will be far greater in glory and power than their former ministries. Their ministries will be protected by God, and anyone who tries to harm them will die by fire that proceeds from their mouths. This again proves the identity of the two witnesses. The enemies who rose against Moses were destroyed by fire (Numbers 16:35), and Elijah had called down fire from heaven to consume the soldiers when they tried to arrest him upon the king's orders (2 Kings 1:10, 12).

The ministry of these two witnesses will only last for 1,260 days. For three and a half years, they will minister in Jerusalem without being harmed (Revelation 11:8). At the end of three and a half years, God will withdraw His protection from them, and the beast, the Antichrist, will overpower them, and kill them.

Their bodies will be left unburied on the streets in Jerusalem for three and a half days, and many will view the dead bodies. The news of their death will spark a national celebration by the Antichrist's nationals and those who have received the mark of the beast.

After three and a half days, these two witnesses, like the Lord Jesus, will be physically resurrected from the dead and then taken up to heaven in the clouds (Revelation 11:11–12). It is most important for us to know that these witnesses are God's warriors during the time of the Antichrist and that God will not let Satan go unchallenged! Throughout biblical and mission history, God has always provided champions for the hour. And He still does!

FINAL WORDS

You are a terror to the kingdom of darkness! As you walk in the Word of the Living God and live a life of humble prayer and obedience, the Lord will use you, your family, and your ministry for His end-time purposes.

I thank the Lord for your having taken this journey with me through the pages of this book. May our Lord anoint you, keep you, and protect you from evil.

The world is waiting for the release of these Special Forces to usher in the Second Coming of Jesus! You are a member of God's Special Forces! Come, Lord Jesus, come!

BIBLIOGRAPHY

_________, *Day of His Power 40 Days Devotional* (Singapore, LoveSingapore, 2005), dated July 10.

_______, *Enrichment Journal.* Springfield, MO: The General Council of the Assemblies of God, 2004).

_________, *The European Union: A Guide for Americans,*" Delegation of the European Commission in the United States, Washington, D.C., 1999.

Alec, Wendy. *Journal of the Unknown Prophet.* Warboys Media, 2002.

Blackaby, Henry, and Richard Blackaby. *Called to Be God's Leader.* Nashville, TN: Thomas Nelson, 2004.

Bonnke, Reinhard. *Evangelism by Fire.* Germany: Full Flame GmbH, 2001.

Bonnke, Reinhard. *Monthly Partners Letter.* Germany: Full Flame, September 2005.

Bounds, E.M. *The Complete Works of E.M. Bounds.* Grand Rapids, MI, 1990.

Bounds, E.M. *Winning the Invisible War.* Whitaker House, 1984.

Cerullo, Morris. *The Last Great Anointing.* Ventura, CA: Renew, Gospel Light, 1999.

DeYoung, Jimmy. "Europe, NATO and the Antichrist." *Israel My Glory,* March/April 2001.

Duewel, Wesley L. *Let God Guide You Daily.* London: Marshall Pickering, 1988.

Duewel, Wesley L. *Mighty Prevailing Prayer.* Grand Rapids, MI: Zondervan, 1990.

Edwards, Brian. *Revival! A People Saturated with God.* Darlington, England: Evangelical Press, 1990; reprint ed. 1994.

Francis, Steven. *Apostolic Relationships and Divine Connections.* Singapore: Rivers of Life Visions International, 2001.

Francis, Steven. *Fragrance Plus Anointing.* Singapore: Rivers of Life Visions International, 2003.

Francis, Steven. *Harvest Glory.* Singapore: Rivers of Life Visions International, 2002.

Franklin, Alan, and Tony Pearce. *EU: Final World Empire.* Oklahoma City, OK: Hearthstone; Southwest Radio Church.

Gossett, Don. *Purity Is Power.* Singapore: BAC Printers, 1992.

Guyon, Jeanne. *Experiencing the Depths of Jesus Christ.* Georgia: SeedSowers, MCMLXXV.

Hagin, Kenneth E. *The Triumphant Church.* Tulsa, OK: Rhema Bible Church, 1993.

Herman, Brigid E. *Creative Prayer.* New York: Harper and Row.

Meyer, Joyce. *The Making of a Leader.* Tulsa, OK: Harrison House, 2001.

Murray, Andrew. *Humility.* New Kensington, PA: Whitaker House, 1982.

Nouwen, Henri J. M. *The Way of the Heart: Desert Spirituality and Contemporary Ministry.* HarperCollins, 1981.

Orton, David. *Snakes in the Temple.* Kent, England: Sovereign World, 2004.

Piper, John. *A Godward Life.* Sisters, OR: Multnomah, 1997.

Pope, Randy. *The Prevailing Church.* Chicago, IL: Moody Press, 2002.

Reagan, Dr. David. "Europe in Bible Prophecy Introduction," article taken from https://lamblion.com/xfiles/publications/magazines/Lamplighter_MayJun01_EuropeanUnion.pdf.

Ricks, Chip. "How to Keep the Pastor You Love," article taken from http://www.bgcworld.org/mag/1005bgc/45.pdf.

Rosenthal, Marvin J. *Zion's Fire* (Zion's Hope, Inc. Orlando, Florida, USA, Nov-Dec, 2004).

Sanders, Oswald J. *Men Who Met God.* London: Marshall, Morgan, & Scott, 1980.

Sanders, Oswald J. *Spiritual Discipleship.* Chicago, IL: Moody Bible Institute, 1990.

Stott, John. *The Message of Romans: The Bible Speaks Today.* Inter-Varsity Press, 1994.

Thompson, Phyllis. *Sadhu Sundar Singh* (OM Publishing, 1992).

Toler, Stan, and Glen Martin. *Survival Skills.* Kansas City, MI: Beacon Hill Press, 2002.

Unger. *The New Unger's Bible Dictionary.* Chicago, IL: Moody Press, 1988.

Vine. *Vine's Expository Dictionary of New Testament Words.* Nashville, TN: Thomas Nelson Publishers, 1985.

Wagner, Peter. *Humility.* Ventura, CA: Regal Books, 2002.

Wagner, Peter. *Radical Holiness for Radical Living.* Colorado Springs, CO: Wagner Institute for Practical Ministry, 1998.

Webster's New Universal Unabridged Dictionary.

Wiersbe, Warren. *The Bible Exposition Commentary.* Colorado Springs, CO: Victor, 2003.

Willis Jr., Avery T., and Henry T. Blackaby. *Experiencing God.* Nashville, TN: Broadman & Holman Publishers, 2002.

WEBSITES CONSULTED

http://www.kidsinministry.com/PropheticChildren.html

http://www.totaldefence.org.sg

http://www.mekong.net/cambodia/mines.htm

http://science.howstuffworks.com/landmine.htm

http://www.catw-ap.org/facts.htm

http://www.icasa.org/uploads/prostitution.pdf

http://www.pucl.org/from-archives/Child/prostitution.htm

http://enrichmentjournal.ag.org/200504/200504_040_sb_lifesaving.cfm

http://www.jesusministries.org

http://www.jesusministries.org/tibetan.html

www.angeltv.org

http://www.singstat.gov.sg/keystats/c2000/wallchart.html#Religion

http://www.omf.org.uk/content.asp?id=8519&cachefixer=

http://money.cnn.com/2006/03/16/news/economy/annie/fortune_annie0317/index.htm

http://www.family.org/pastor/pfmarried/a0016832.cfm

www.eurunion.org

http://galileo.rice.edu/gal/urban/html

http://www.answers.com/topic/holy-roman-emperor-2

http://en.wikipedia.org/wiki/CD

http://www.tscpulpitseries.org/english/1990s/ts940613.html

http://en.wikipedia.org/wiki/War_horse

http://www.factmonster.com/ipka/A0004737.html

AUDIO-VISUAL: DVD

Hathaway, David. *The Rape of Europe.* United Kingdom: Prophetic Vision, 2004. http://www.propheticvision.org.uk

Alan Franklin and Tony Pearce, *EU: Final World Empire,* a video program produced by Hearthstone and distributed in the USA by Southwest Radio Church in Oklahoma City, Oklahoma.

Steven Francis Ministries
409 Polkville Road, Shelby,
North Carolina 28150, USA.
Tel: +1 704 406 9090

Mailing Address:
P.O. Box 1027
Kings Mountain, NC 28086